JOURNAL IV, 1979–1985

MIRCEA ELIADE

JOURNAL IV
1979–1985

Translated from the Romanian by Mac Linscott Ricketts

Epilogue by Wendy Doniger

THE UNIVERSITY OF CHICAGO PRESS

Chicago and London

The University of Chicago Press, Chicago 60637
The University of Chicago Press, Ltd., London
© 1990 by Georgette Eliade
© 1990 by The University of Chicago
All rights reserved. Published 1990
Printed in the United States of America

99 98 97 96 95 94 93 92 91 90 54321

∞ The paper used in this publication meets the minimum requirements of the American National Standard for Information Sciences—Permanence of Paper for Printed Library Materials, ANSI Z39.48-1984

Library of Congress Cataloging-in-Publication Data

Eliade, Mircea, 1907–
    Journal IV, 1979–1985.

    Includes index.
    1. Eliade, Mircea, 1907– —Diaries.   I. Title.
II. Title: Journal 4, 1979–1985.   III. Title: Journal
four, 1979–1985.
BL43.E4A3 1990   291'.092   [B]   89-5071
ISBN 0-226-20414-6 (alk. paper)

Contents

Translator's Note

It gives me great personal satisfaction to see this volume of Mircea Eliade's journal excerpts, the third to be published in English thus far, appearing in a translation made directly from the Romanian original. The two earlier volumes were made from the French translation published by Gallimard in Paris, and hence risk the dangers to which any double translation is prone. A fourth English volume, for the earliest years available, 1945–1955 (to be called Volume I), will be published next, also in a direct translation from the Romanian.

In the present volume, material supplied by the translator has been enclosed in brackets. So also have the selections Eliade made for this volume out of his "Datebook" (apparently a small appointment calendar), which he wanted to distinguish from selections made from his journal notebooks or loose pages on which he had made journal entries and notes.

Numerous references are made herein to *Histoire* III and IV, books on which Eliade was working during this period. The full title of the work is *Histoire des croyances et des idées religieuses,* published in three volumes by Payot in Paris (1976–1983) and in English by the University of Chicago Press (1978–85). As published, they bear Arabic numbers (1,2,3), but since Eliade always designated them by Roman numerals, they appear that way in the present text. Volume IV, for which Eliade seems to have written two or more chapters and requested other scholars to contribute additional chapters, has not been published due to the difficulties of completing the work since his death in 1986.

In this volume of his journal, Eliade speaks repeatedly and almost pathetically of wanting to finish his autobiography. Volume II of that work, for the years 1937–1960, was published in 1988 by the University of Chicago Press, although the work was not finished to the point Eliade had planned. The present volume of journal excerpts, as well as Volume III, already in print, are all the more valuable in that they deal with the years that Eliade was unable to cover in his *Autobiography.*

This last volume of Mircea Eliade's journal excerpts is, inevitably, a sad chronicle. Time, always his enemy, is overtaking him and he knows it. There are repeated references to pains, fatigue, ennui, loss of powers—the author has not expunged or tried to gloss over his suffering from the many physical infirmities that beset him in the last years; but at the same time there shines forth from these pages an indefatigable spirit, a mind fully alert and creative as ever, a drive and determination to finish all the self-appointed tasks. Even in these final years, Mircea Eliade remains, like the myth-figures he taught us to interpret, paradigmatic to the end, setting a standard none of us, his former students, will ever be able to even half-approximate.

While the final responsibility for this translation remains my own, I wish to express deep and sincere appreciation for the help I received from Christinel Eliade, who went over the entire manuscript with meticulous and loving care and corrected many initial errors, and to India Cooper for her conscientious and skillful editorial labors.

Mac Linscott Ricketts
Louisburg College

CHICAGO, *7 January 1979*
    We returned yesterday afternoon, after a night spent in the same hotel in Mexico City. The cold temperature was an unpleasant surprise, but we are glad, nevertheless, to be home.
    This morning I try to put the finishing touches to some notes from Yucatán; I wrote with a pencil in great haste, and they would have become completely illegible in a week's time.
    In the afternoon, an interview with a young Japanese woman, Myie Uchida, editor of a bimonthly magazine at first sight very impressive: two hundred pages! Questions about religion and desacralization, Shinto and Zen, American young people, etc. An hour lost. And I had promised myself I wouldn't give any more interviews!
    Letters: Barbu Brezianu and Edith Silbermann. This evening: dinner at the Kitagawas'.

8 January
    A day lost going through correspondence and books accumulated at Swift Hall during our absence: a whole box full.
    I find out that a good part of the last number (but which?) of *Secolul 20* is devoted to me, and that excerpts from *L'Épreuve du labyrinthe,* translated into Romanian, have appeared in *Luceafărul,* filling a whole page. But the editors have not thought to send me copies.

(For my "collection," of course, and especially for the bibliography which Allen and Doeing are preparing, because for many years now I haven't read what is written about me.)

I receive some ten books which I shall not have time to read, except one: Ewart H. Cousins, *Bonaventura and the Coincidence of Opposites* (the problem of the *coincidentia oppositorum* will fascinate me till the end of my life). Nevertheless, I shall have to dictate letters of thanks to the authors.

This evening I try to write those several pages about my "philosophy" promised last summer to Amzăr. Impossible. And yet, I don't dare take up something that interests me: the interrupted novella, or the chapter on Meso-American religions for *Histoire* III, or the revision of the notes from Yucatán and Guatemala.

[*Datebook*
10 January: letters to Douglas Allen, Gallimard. 11 January: letters to Al. Zub, N. Catauy, G. Anca, Sorin [Alexandrescu]. Correct (for the French translation) chapter 14 of *Aminitiri*. 12 January: Receive the first copy of *A History of Religious Ideas*, volume 1, and the second edition of *Fôret interdite.*]

13 January
It snowed all night. The airport is closed again. Streets blocked.

14 January
It snowed again last night also. The snow is piled as high as in the winter of 1917 in Bucharest. But now the sky is blue and glassy.

15 January
Now and then I am in perfect accord with Karl Barth. For example, with this statement: "What kind of God is the one whose existence must be demonstrated?"

[*Datebook*
16 January: letters: Ioan Culianu, D. Allen, Rocquet. 19 January: I begin the review about Spinoza for the *Journal of Religion,* promised

to the editor. 20 January: I finish the review article: eight pages of manuscript. Evening: Ricoeur, at our place. Letters: V. Ieurunca, D. Hăulică.]

21 January

I begin writing the interview for *Le Monde*.

23 January

This evening, for dinner at our place, Siegfried and Joachim Unseld; just the four of us. An informal dinner, since I know this will please Siegfried: caviar, Manchurian fish roe, champagne, cognac. We find out many interesting things. He insists I begin preparations for the first volumes of my *Werke* (in German translation).

24 January

At 4:15, Siegfried's lecture. But the streets were packed with snow, certain doors had been locked, and so the hall (fortunately not large) was almost empty. We dine with the members of the German department at the Quadrangle Club, then we come to our apartment for cognac and whiskey.

Speaking yesterday with Siegfried about the Nobel Prize, he told me that, of course, Ernst Jünger would have merited it long ago, but had it been awarded to him, a "planetary uproar" would have erupted. Not because Jünger was once a Nazi; everyone knows he was not. But he espouses "conservative-aristocratic" ideas, those of the Samurai.

25 January

Seminar: *Beowulf*. I finish the interview for *Le Monde*.

[*Datebook*

26 January: As usual, letters, but I won't mention them here. 27 January: In the evening, at our place: Jonathan [Z. Smith], Ricoeur, Wendy O'Flaherty, David Tracy. 28 January: Letter to Dumézil.]

1 February

Letter to Michel Waldberg, accompanying the text of the *Le Monde* interview. As usual, I'm dissatisfied. But, on the one hand, I have too many things to do and to finish urgently; on the other hand, short (i.e., precipitate, "specialized") interviews no longer interest me.

3 February

I reread *Nouăsprezece trandafiri* [Nineteen roses]. I write—and succeed in transcribing—another four or five pages.

[Translator's note: *Nineteen Roses* was begun at Eygalières, France, in August 1978; see *Journal* III, August 6, 7, 9, September 2, 8, etc.]

4 February

From morning till 5:00 P.M., no desire to work. I begin to write at 5:30. In three hours, I write twelve pages.

5 February

Exceptionally cold; $-8°F$. But the light is superb. I write all day: eleven pages. I correct and transcribe five pages.

7 February

This evening, seminar on Gesar; almost three hours. How exciting it would have been if even some of the members of the seminar had read the admirable monograph of R. A. Stein, *L'Epopée et le Bard au Tibet*. I show them the voluminous (one thousand pages) and controversial book of Matthias Hermanns (S.V.D.), *Gling König Ge Sar* (Regensburg, 1965). No one ventures to ask to borrow it. (I say to myself that probably I'm the only one who has read it—and not just in Chicago!)

Today I resumed work on *Nouăsprezece trandafiri*. I transcribe ten pages and write eight.

8 February

I don't feel very well. Seven pages transcribed. Letter to Rocquet.

9 February

Don't feel well (stomach—but maybe it's something else). Can't continue the transcribing.

10 February
Although ill, I write nine pages.

11 February
I write all day: fifteen pages.

12 February
Not a single page!
I remembered about *Bêtes, hommes et dieux,* the very successful book of Ossendowsky, which I read in adolescence. I believe it was there that I first learned about the Mongol myth of Gesar. Then, a few years later, I read the translation of Alexandra David-Neel and her adopted son, a lama whose name escapes me now. But only the reading of Stein's book revealed to me the importance of this "epic." I wonder why the book hasn't been successful. . . .

14 February
For two days, I've written nothing. This evening: seminar on Meister Eckhart. (As Titu Maiorescu used to say: "And how much more would remain to be said!")

17 February
Yesterday, I wrote six pages (but I'm not sure I'll keep them all). Today, seven.

19 February
Last night we dined at the Quadrangle Club with Ravi Ravindra, professor of physics and religion at Dalhousie University, Halifax, Nova Scotia. He informed me that the Threshold Foundation has granted me half of the Threshold Award, $25,000, the other half being given to a biologist.
There will be a reception at New York or Paris; I shall have to say a few words. In principle, I shall be obliged to write an essay which will be published, etc.

20 February

Yesterday and today I've written ten pages and transcribed the same number.

One of my students in the seminar asks me why I am *not* interested in dreams. I reply that, on the contrary, they fascinate me. Between 1955 and 1956 I recorded every morning whole series of dreams. Rereading them later, it seemed to me I discerned certain "messages." There are several dreams which I have not forgotten: for example, the one of the library in Bucharest, in which I saw how it was decimated, how whole collections (Papini, the history of religions, India) disappeared, one after another. And the one about the amphitheater: when I arrive at the top, I realize it is empty and partially in ruins. (The dream was repeated several times, but the ending was not always sad.)

21 February

Last night, seminar on the Graal. Rather interesting.

I write three pages and transcribe ten.

22 February

Because he asks me *how* to compose his paper on the subject of death, I tell him that the history of religions presents *collective* conceptions about death (mythologies, rituals, beliefs), not the personal meditations of philosophers. These latter become intelligible and important only after the reader knows the former and after he has familiarized himself with several theologies of death.

I doubt that I convinced him. Besides, at his age and with his knowledge, he wouldn't dare undertake such an approach. I advise him to choose a "cultural area" and study it exhaustively. "But which one?" he asks me, troubled. "I know that India interests you. Concentrate on Indian conceptions. Or else on only one aspect: rituals, myths."

He left pensive, after having thanked me somewhat absently. He was wondering, probably, how many pages he'd have to read. . . .

25 February

I've managed to write a few pages every day. Today a surprise: twenty!

Last night, went to see Anne Rose Kitagawa in *The Mikado*.

26 February

Superb day. Sunny (with a full eclipse announced; I didn't see it, however). I write eighteen pages.

28 February

Last night's seminar: on Australia. From now on, it ought to become more and more interesting. We are concentrating on archaic religions.

Today I wrote fifteen pages, and I *finished* it. I correct and transcribe twenty pages; am up to page 318.

1 March

Bad night. I transcribe; have reached page 330.

2 March

I write and post many letters (E. Silbermann, Siegfried, etc.), enclosing in each envelope a copy of Leslie Maitland's interview from the *New York Times* [4 February 1979].

5 March

In the past few days I've written some twelve letters. I correct the typed text of *Nouăsprezece trandafiri*. I have dedicated it to Ileana and Ioan Cuşa. They will, I am sure, understand why.

7 March

I send *Nouăsprezece trandafiri* to Ierunca, Matei Calinescu, and Edith Silbermann. This time, I'm waiting impatiently to receive their responses. Not that I doubt the literary success of the novel, but I wonder if the *message,* so skillfully camouflaged, will be understood.

Last night, seminar on the Iroquois and the Bantu.

9 March

. . .And so, I've reached the age of seventy-two. I can hardly believe it. . . . How happy I'd be if I didn't have to write *Histoire III!* My big mistake: I started too late to write this book, which I wanted to be the *last* in my scientific corpus.

13 March

I lost several hours today searching through drawers, on top of the desk, and among files of manuscripts for all the *Journal* notes written this winter. And I'm not sure I found them all. Why did I stop keeping the *Journal* in a notebook, as I did between 1945 and 1971?

14 March

Yesterday evening, the last seminar, and probably the best. Larry Sullivan, on the Trickster. When we were leaving, I said to Wendy that the text should be published in *History of Religions*. The only difficulty: we decided from the outset not to publish articles by our students until they pass their doctorates.

16 March

I do nothing but answer letters and send copies of my books to several critics and historians in Romania.

This evening we dine with the Philipsons at the Chinese restaurant. We evoke meetings with Siegfried Unseld, and so forth. . . .

17 March

A former student of mine, Norman Girardot, comes from Notre Dame to see me. Troubles: his contract at the university has not been renewed. And I realize very well why: Norman knows too many different things, he's interested in too many "subjects" (Taoism, alchemy, folklore, literary imagination, etc.). He tells me, among other things, about his "prestige" among students because he has known and *lived* that fabulous epoch—now almost mythicized—of the discovery of drugs: 1960–1965. Students ask him: "What was it like then?" As I can imagine young people asked the first oceanic navigators, or the survivors of the Terror, or the veterans returned from Moscow with the remnants of *La Grande Armée*.

18 March

Warm. Already summer. I write five letters.

19 March

I send to Professor Giulia Piccaluga my article from the A. Brelich *Festschrift* ["Druids, Astronomers, and Head-Hunters," in *Perennitas: Studi in onore di Angelo Brelich* (Rome, 1980)]. I wrote it because I had promised it and because I wanted to honor, through the presentation of a text (even a mediocre one), a savant with whom I have seldom been in agreement, but whom I have admired. And his book, *Gli Eroi Greci*—how much I learned from reading it!

[*Datebook*

20–23 March: I write an immense number of letters, meet with students, and prepare the dossier on Islam.]

24 March

I begin the chapter, "Mahomet et l'essor de l'Islam" [Muhammad and the unfolding of Islam].

31 March

Moving a stack of files from one shelf to another, I come across a dossier made of reddish cardboard (I had it already in Paris!) on which I had written "Australia." I was sure I had incinerated all those materials, with the exception of the latest bibliographies, immediately after the appearance of *Australian Religions* (Cornell University Press, 1973). I carried several sacks of papers, full of files, notebooks, slips of paper, note cards, bibliographic references, lesson plans, etc., to the basement. I *had* to proceed this way with these materials (as well as with those on shamanism, etc.). With so many kilograms of paper lying about, I wasn't able to find anything. Already, I wonder *what I'll do,* how—and where: to Paris?—shall I transport those twenty-some kilos of correspondence, original manuscripts of literary writings in Romanian, and folders in which I have collected my articles and—as many as possible—studies and articles about me. And we are alone—the two of us—here on this campus. *Anything* could happen, at any time. And those five thousand pages of the *Journal*. . . . Instead of attending to my work, I suffer from melancholy provoked, as usual, by . . . what I *must* do now, immediately. I give away books all the time, but this is no solution; I receive others. For the time being, I fill the wastebasket with my old resumés and notes on Australia.

2 April

In my library in front of me, a whole shelf is occupied with file folders, notes, manuscripts, and documentary materials (various articles received over the past fifteen years) relative to the projected monograph *Le Centre du monde*. Although I doubt I shall ever undertake to write it in its entirety, I still preserve this documentary archive—and continually add new materials to it. Today I transferred some twelve or thirteen packets to my desk, in search of an article by Werner Müller. In this fashion I found that file in which, last May, I collected a good part of the cards for the index to *Histoire* II. I looked for it at that time for several days. I had to redo the work in New York and Paris in June.

18 April

Jean Montalbetti from Radio France (France-Culture) comes to interview me for a program in a series of twenty: "Les Universités et l'universel." He had told Christinel on the telephone that the whole thing would last five minutes and that the questions would bear upon the history of religions curriculum at the University of Chicago. Actually, the interview lasted fifty minutes. The young man asked me all sorts of questions about my activities and beliefs (of the genre *L'Épreuve du labyrinthe*). Bored, annoyed, I answered him offhandedly in an atrocious French.

25 April

I had agreed to speak at the faculty-student luncheon about *A History of Religious Ideas*. I manage to say a few interesting things:

morphology-typology-history; today we are *not* in a decadent Alexandrian era, but in one comparable to that of Herodotus (when, for the first time, the Greeks discovered and tried to understand archaic and barbarian societies); the history of religions could influence the Western cultural milieu as psychoanalysis did fifty to sixty years ago.

26 April

This evening, Brutus Coste telephones me from New York: he asks me to head the Romanian-American committee for the freeing of Father Calciu. It seems that the Patriarch and two metropolitans are in the United States now, explaining and illustrating ''religious freedom'' in Romania. This piece of information humiliates and exasperates me: the church itself persecuting the last Christians and agreeing to be the instrument of the Terror!

Of course, I agree to be president of the committee. Probably this will cost me my ''rehabilitation'' in Romania—but I could not do otherwise.

27 April

I write a long letter to S., explaining why I cannot accept his suggestion (following his discussions with V.C.) of visiting the homeland. Five pages. I have retained a copy (photocopied).

28 April

I write to Cazenave (Radio France-Culture) that I cannot participate in the colloquium at Cordoba (in October).

I finish the chapter on Muhammad (sixty-two pages in manuscript). Still to be written: the critical bibliography and *état des questions*.

1 May

Superb day. At 4:00: Marjorie Reeves's lecture, ''Dante and Gioacchino da Fiore.'' I had read with interest her voluminous work, *The Influence of Prophecy in the Later Middle Ages*. Her lecture reminded me of my youth, when I discovered Gioacchino through the studies and letters of Ernesto Buonaiuti. Since then, 1925–1927, my ''passion'' for the Calabrian abbot has never abated.

I take advantage of the subject chosen by Marjorie Reeves to ask her if, in the famous verses

> Voi ch'avete l'intelletti sani
> Guardate la dottrina che s'asconde
> Sotto il velame degli versi sani . . .

she can discover an indication of Gioacchino's "prophecies." (The question has tormented me from youth.) But Marjorie Reeves does not venture to assert anything precise, although the hypothesis does not strike her as absurd.

[*Datebook*

2–4 May: Letters, letters. In order to rest, I gather material for the second chapter on Islam into file folders. But I won't begin to write till I get to Paris.]

5 May

I correct the manuscript, "Entretiens," for *L'Express* [published 31 August 1979]. There is a great deal I could add, make more specific, or nuance. But what would be the use? I hope that my future readers will read my books, not the interviews.

7 May

I decide suddenly to telegraph Fritz Kroeger, informing him that I shall not be able to deliver the promised lecture, "The Experience of the Sacred," on 21 June. The reason given—an operation for a cataract on my right eye—is only half-invented. American opthalmologists insist on it. . . . I'm following the advice of the ophthalmologist in Paris—drops, etc.—but for the time being I don't see much result.

In any event, the telegram has taken a load off my shoulders. I'd have had to begin work on the lecture as soon as we arrived in Paris, 21 or 22 May. And the subject no longer interests me. I don't understand why I accepted the invitation last autumn.

9 May

I begin *In Search of History,* by Theodore H. White, an enormous autobiography which Christinel finished reading a few days ago. The life of a family of poor Jewish immigrants from Russia, in Boston. I remember about my childhood: Strada Melodiei and all the other streets (Calea Moşilor, etc.), populated by well-to-do Christian families and a few families of poor Jews. The vacant lots where we played together. . . .

11 May

We dine at the Crossants,' with that Indian couple who have wanted for a long time to meet me. Christinel comes at 10:30, after *Fidelio*. We recall the performance of sixteen or seventeen years ago, when we were guests of John Nef. That unforgettable chorus of prisoners. . . .

12 May

A whole day for myself! And the weather's incomparably beautiful. But at 2:00 a group of students come by for "information" relative to the examinations.

I write a large number of bibliographic notes: "Indologica I," for *History of Religions* [20, no. 3 (Winter 1980)]. Later I'll regret the time lost on such trifles. But I want to say something laudatory about Tucci's *Opera Minora* and the admirable critical edition of Gnoli, *The Gilgit Manuscript*.

This evening we dine with Mary Stevenson at the Agora Restaurant.

13 May

I finished, after a great effort, "Indologica I." But only a few lines about the books of Lommel and Gonda (and I might have said so much!). Then, between 4:00 and 5:00, thunderstorm.

This evening, with Dr. and Mrs. Edward Levi, at the Chinese restaurant, House of Hunan.

14 May

Yesterday and today, preparations for the "work in Paris." I arrange for the mailing of several packages of books and manuscripts.

Today, letters. We decide that one of our students (in history of religions), Catherine Bell, will live in our apartment during the summertime.

15 May

Superb day. We fly to New York. Surprise: upset stomach. Impossible to understand *why*.

NEW YORK, 17 May

Cocktails with a few colleagues from the French Institute.

18 May

I try to prepare the address which I must give at the Threshold Foundation luncheon.

At 6:00: Costel Teodoru.

19 May

At 11:00: appointment and lunch; we meet the Iranian prince who finances the Threshold Foundation, plus Walter Kaufmann and Roger Lipsey. I read a short text in which I repeat whole passages from various recent articles and interviews.

In the evening we dine at Tantzi and Brutus Coste's apartment.

PARIS, 22 May

We arrive at 8:30 A.M. Waiting for us at the airport are Ioan Cuşa and Maiza. The sky is overcast and drizzling, and it's cold.

At home, a surprise: the two downstairs apartments are being renovated. I try for half an hour to fall asleep: impossible! Noise, hammering on the walls.

23 May

At 2:30 Sorin Popa comes to see me. He brings me books by Victor Ion Popa and a number of presents: some ceramic beads from Ilfov, painted eggs from Agapia and Horezu monasteries, soil from Agapia, a few stones from the shore of the Black Sea, etc. His little son sends me a dozen pigeon feathers, and his daughter a gourd. He shows me photographs: himself with his wife and children. He spent sixteen years in prison after four years at war: sentenced to twenty-five years at hard labor for "a plot against the security of the Fatherland." He says he was given a passport thanks to my letters and the several books (*Histoire* I and II, *Traité*, etc.) which I had sent him. He showed them to someone at Security and obtained a passport. (Moreover, he has a good opinion of Security. He says that all the men are well educated— doctors, engineers, professors, university graduates, etc.—trained to gather information about the "mood" of their respective professional groups. The Security man who gave him the passport told him to have a talk with me and find out "under what conditions I'd consent to come to the country."

25 May

I begin transcribing the notations for the *Journal* for 1973 (some from the *Datebook*), the majority of them written on pieces of paper of different sizes; some have appeared already in *Limite* and *Revista şcriitorilor români*. I spend a considerable amount of time classifying them and identifying, at least approximately, when they were written. Perhaps it would have been better if I had arranged them, without chronological order, in the form of *Notebooks* or *Carnets*.

This evening we telephone Corina. She still hasn't received her passport. V. C. has promised her he'll "see to it."

26 May

From 2:00 till 3:00, with Sorin Popa. He brings me the sketch which Victor Ion Popa made of me in 1937 or 1938. At 4:00 I go to *L'Herne*. Tacou shows me *Andronic et le serpent* [French translation of *Şarpele*, 1937]. The cover is beautiful. But on the inside cover page, the title is *Le Serpent!*

At 7:00 come Marius Robescu (whom I'd never met) and Eugen Simion (whom I saw the last time here in Paris two years ago). "Literary" discussion: the situation in Romania. The four of us dine at the Algerian restaurant on the corner (mediocre), then we continue our discussion at our apartment until almost midnight. I have noted several particulars on sheets of paper which will serve for the writing of the *Journal*.

At 9:30, telephone call from Sorin.

29 May

Meeting with Cioran at the Café Escorial. As usual, scintillating, pessimistic, discreet (he never talks about himself, his "successes," the book he's working on). Among other things, he tells me (he found it out from Taubes, or from others) that in West Berlin today I am better known (more "popular") as a writer than as a historian of religions (which doesn't please me: my ideal is to be known "totally").

In the evening we dine with the Ieruncas.

30 May

A quarter of an hour lost standing in line at the post office on place des Abbesses in order to claim a registered packet: a volume of poetry by an Italian author, probably young, unknown. I page through the book on the way home. Depressingly mediocre poems. Then, great sadness: the hopes which that unknown poet has, certainly, pinned on my response. . . .

[*Datebook*

2 June: Meetings: at 5:00 with Grigorescu; at 6:00 with E. Simion at the Cluny; at 8:00 with Cioran.]

3 June

Sorin Popa writes me from Vienna something he didn't dare tell me in Paris: at our first meeting, on learning he had no money to pay his hotel bill, I gave him five hundred francs. He was happy and assured me he would pay it back, in lei, at Bucharest, to Corina. A half hour after he left, probably on the Metro, his billfold was stolen, with the money and papers (except his passport and train ticket). When he came to see me the second time, he said nothing about it, lest I think he was expecting me to lend him more. From the consulate he obtained one-hundred francs, with which he paid the hotel.

[*Datebook*

5 June: at 3:30 Grigorescu comes to check with me his translation of the *Autobiography (Memoire* I). It is, of course, "correct," but Greg has the tendency to "explain," to add information in notes.]

6 June

From a letter of Culianu, forwarded from Chicago, I learn that Furio Jesi has devoted a chapter of calumnies and insults to me in his book that has come out recently, *Cultura di destra* [Culture of the right]. I learned long ago that Jesi considers me an anti-Semite, fascist, Iron Guardist, etc. Probably he accuses me also of Buchenwald. And yet, he proposed himself as translator for my *Histoire* for Rizzoli. This past year I found out ("inside information") that he allegedly said: "So long as I'm director of this series [on the history of religions], Eliade's book will not appear!" I conveyed this piece of information to Jean-Luc Pidoux-Payot, requesting him to see what was happening. Pidoux wrote to Rizzoli. After some time I receive a letter from Furio Jesi in which he apologizes for the delay in the translation: the university chair he has been offered, the organization of courses, etc., have kept him from beginning the translation. But he assures me that, with the assistance of a team of students, he will finish the translation very soon. . . .

And now, suddenly, the perfidous attack in *Cultura di destra*. From such an individual I can expect anything. I shall ask Pidoux to intervene: (1) to allow me to check the translation (he is capable of falsifying the text in order to make me come out . . . a Nazi!), and (2) to send me his preface. It makes no difference to me if he abuses me in his book (I shan't read it, and therefore I won't respond to it); but I can't consent to being insulted in the preface of my own book!

7 June

A visit from the Spanish editor of my most recent books: *Histoire* and several others (Editiones Cristiandad). He has big plans. He hopes that my books will be as successful as several recent volumes of theology. . . .

This evening for dinner at our place: Doina and Virgil Tănase.

8 June

Several weeks ago I received a letter, forwarded from Chicago, from a woman, S. P., who informed me that she had written poetry (in

Romanian and English) and a novel (in French), but had been unable to publish them. Day before yesterday I received a large envelope with some two-hundred sheets of paper, handwritten on both sides and incorrectly numbered. "I didn't type it, because I couldn't find a typewriter with French diacritical marks. If it is published, I want it to appear under my old name, S. B." For a moment I was tempted to return the manuscript unopened. But I was impressed by the fact that she had chosen the cheapest paper sold in the United States, and some of the pages had school exercises written on the backs. Such "economizing" spoke to me of dire poverty. I began the reading—with difficulty, because the pages were numbered haphazardly. Depressing account of months spent in Israel; terrible experience at New York. Unfortunately, I don't see who would publish it.

12 June

At 3:30, Grigorescu. This endless checking of a text in a French which is exemplary, but whose tempo I don't recognize. At 6:30, Paleologu. I ask him about the homeland, especially about literature and literary criticism there. . . . He regrets that I didn't continue *Oceanografie*.

Dinner at Dehollain's, with Cioran.

14 June

From 2:30 to 5:00, at the Institut de France for the reception of Georges Dumézil into the academy. Apprised by G. D., we arrived a half hour early and walked on the quai, waiting for the door to be opened. Fortunately, it wasn't raining.

We entered for the first time beneath that famous cupola. G. D. read his address (about the historian of the Third Republic whose chair he will occupy). Claude Lévi-Strauss responded. Then, the reception at Collège de France.

15 June

Ioana Miereanu tells me this, after spending a month with her parents at a village in Gorj: magic is practiced a great deal and is taken seriously not only by "those who go to church," but even more so by "Socialist functionaries." What an interesting subject for research: magic in a socialist state!

From 2:30 to 5:30 at the Café Cluny. I correct the last chapter of the *Autobiography* translated by Grigorescu.

16 June

Zed, the Sanskritist who will translate *Le Yoga* into Serbo-Croatian, comes to see me.

19 June

Summer seems to be coming. . . .

This evening, at Grigorescu's, with the Ieruncas, to see the film *Bucharest, 1928*.

22 June

At 7:30, at the Tacous': reception for the marriage of their daughter, the beautiful Florence, to the son of Claude Mauriac. At 8:00, with G. Dumézil at the home of his son, the doctor. Splendid apartment. At dinner, Claude Lévi-Strauss—very charming toward me. But we didn't talk much. Only in the taxi did I realize I'd taken Lévi-Strauss's raincoat by mistake.

Corina arrived at 9:30. Christinel and Ioan Culianu went to Orly to meet her.

26 June

I read the correspondence of Basil Munteanu. Depressed by the memories it stirs up. And that famous doctoral thesis of his, on which he worked for twenty years and never published because, according to his wife, the manuscript was lost when they fled their home (in the spring of 1940).

[*Datebook*

28 June: We eat dinner with the Dumézils, at the Yugoslavian restaurant.]

29 June

This evening with Corina at the Ieruncas'.

30 June

Charlotte and Gordon Collier arrive. In the evening we all (including Corina too) dine at the restaurant Le Relais Normand.

2 July

Invited by Claude Gallimard, we take lunch—Eugène Ionesco, Cioran, and I—at a neighborhood restaurant. Eugène confesses to me that for a year he has been unable to read anything except histories of the modern theater. He is seeking to see how he will be judged by history. (To Cioran he confessed on the telephone that at least once a week he is preoccupied with the question: what will remain after my death?)

3 July

Constantin Sporea sends me a photocopy of a page of the catalogue of the University of Regensburg, the *Religionswissenschaft Section*. One of the seminars is entitled: "Mircea Eliade: Nicht Ontologie, nicht Emanzipation, aber das Heilige." For a title, that's not so bad!

4 July

Barbăneagră relates to me what Jean Servier said to him recently: that from Israel they have received precise instructions that I am to be criticized and attacked as a fascist, etc. Jean Servier, says Barbăneagră, was indignant. . . . I believe it, but there's nothing to be done.

At 4:00 that foreign Sinologist with the large paunch comes to see me. He has a whole briefcase full of manuscripts. He tries to persuade me that some interpretation or other of a certain "master" is false.

[*Datebook*

5 July: I see Robert Gallimard and C. Tacou.]

16 July

La Baronne d'Oberkirch wrote in 1789: "Je demande seulement pour mon gendre une haute naissance, car il y a remède à tout, sauf au manque de naissance" (*Mémoires,* Paris, 1970, 32). [For my son-in-law I demand only a high birth, because there is a remedy for everything save a lack of birth.]

17 July

I receive a letter from one Alain Volut, who introduces himself as a tightrope dancer (*danseur de corde*). He explains: "I walk on the rope, but that which touches me most and that which I work at and practice on the tightrope are above all the movements of a dance, *my* dance. This involves my body and soul sometimes in 'dances,' or 'voyages,' that are very important and 'grave' for me. I should like very much to study that more closely." He asks me for information, suggestions, and bibliography about the origins of the symbolism and beliefs relative to the tightrope dance. He declares that for him "the rope dance is not an exercise in skill nor a circus act, but a very important realization of our relationship to the world, to the earth, to the sky, to gravity, to different points of view."

18 July

We dine at Rocquet's.

Useless to record here how hard it is for me to work on *Histoire* III. The fact is, I content myself with reading files, underlining (how many times does this make?) certain passages from my notes of several years ago.

19 July

At 11:45, at the ophthalmologist's. The cataract progresses, but rather slowly (thanks to the drops from Japan?). At any rate, I will change lenses again. I read with some effort, but, nevertheless, I *read.*

I shall have to conclude *Histoire* III with the chapters on Islam, the Renaissance, and the Reformation.

20 *July*

Drowsy. I reread *Nouăsprezece trandafiri* and am much moved.

21 *July*

Last night's dream: I leave home with the manuscript of a study on which I had worked several months, to make a photocopy of it. I come to a strange garden or park in the vicinity of the office where the manuscript is to be photocopied. A well-dressed man is there, with many small animals around him. I don't know why, but I fold the manuscript and press it together, reducing it to the size of a sandwich, and try, for fun, to threaten a little rat with it. But the animal takes hold of the packet with his mouth and won't let go. Although he isn't biting or chewing it, I observe that the manuscript is getting smaller. Impossible to pull it out of the rat's mouth. I have nothing handy with which to hit it. Alarmed, I beg the elegant gentleman, who is standing directly in front of me, to stab the rat. He replies that *here* he does not have the right to fire a revolver (?). I watch desperately as my manuscript disappears. Very soon there is nothing left in my hand but a narrow strip of paper, a few millimeters wide. Only then does the rat let loose of it—and he goes away. I was desperate. I had lost an important text on which I had worked many months; and I hadn't saved any notes, not even the note cards. . . . I started toward the office of the photocopier, at my wits' end. Fortunately, a few moments later I woke up. But for a long time I couldn't go back to sleep. I realized that the dream constituted a "message," but I didn't succeed in deciphering it.

23 *July*

C. Poghirc comes to see me. Furious about the imbecility of the "authorities" in the homeland, who have not allowed his wife and child to come to Padova, where he has been professor for three years. *He,* Poghirc emphasizes, who for fifteen years traveled around the globe several times, attending conferences, holding courses and lectures—and always returned. Probably an informer provoked suspicion. On account of this, he has decided to remain permanently in the West. He talks also about the campaign against me in Italy, provoked by F. Jesi. The aim: to eliminate me from among the favorites for the Nobel Prize.

24 July

After 9:00, Ben Corlaciu and his wife (whom I hadn't met) come to see us. Ben C. seems just as thin now as he was three years ago on the Esplanada Trocadero after a fifteen-day hunger strike. He does almost all the talking. He has received the fifteen-hundred-page manuscript of his journal from the homeland. The selection of two to three hundred pages, typed, interested no Romanian in Paris other than C. V. Gheorghiu. Of course, C. V. G. suggested that he write an autobiographical novel (centering on those twenty-six days of his hunger strike) in which he could introduce elements from the journal. B. C. hopes to finish the novel in September.

[*Datebook*

25 July: Antoine Faivre. As usual, polite, erudite, and yet imaginative. I am moved by his admiration and love for Henry Corbin. Tears welled up in his eyes when I pronounced Henry's name.]

26 July

Hot. At 3:00 Grigorescu comes. In the evening we eat dinner at Gaby and Jean Gouillard's.

27–28 July

Hot. The clear sky of summer. I should record what Corina tells me about Romania.

29 July

I finish transcribing fragments of the *Journal* for 1974.

1 August

I finish compiling the article on myth for *Civiltà delle macchine*. (I don't understand why I ever agreed to write it.)

2 August

Corina leaves for Amsterdam, where Sorin and Liliana are waiting for her. Only now will she begin to travel *really* (and in an automobile, as she likes).

This evening, for dinner, Marie-France and Gelu Ionescu. I find myself suddenly living in three or four worlds.

4 August

The beautiful weather continues. Summer days, with no trace of melancholy. I do nothing; this state of "freedom" makes me feel ten or fifteen years younger. *Everything* can begin from the beginning.

LYON, 5 August

We spend the whole day with Oani and Lily. The city fascinates me more and more, as I discover it: the façades of those buildings, noble and austere at the same time, on the banks of the two rivers, and the houses which rise above them, climbing high up the hillsides. . . .

Their house is situated on a hill, close to that palace in the midst of a park which today belongs to the city. The veranda of their house extends well out into the yard.

We ride around in the car until 9:00 P.M. Oani and Lily are distressed that now, in August, the "famous restaurants" are all closed. We have an excellent dinner at the Villa de Rome.

EYGALIÈRES, 6 August

We leave Lyon at 5:00. In two hours we are in Avignon, where Ioan Cuşa is waiting for us. I should have discovered Provence fifty years ago when I used to like to ramble around the countryside, especially the Carpathians, for whole weeks, without getting bored or tired.

9 August

Superb weather. Am reading Jules Verne. Each day I bathe in the swimming pool. But I'm afraid to stay out in the sun very long; and if, like all the others, I were to put a "summer hat" on my head, I'd have the feeling I was in disguise.

Yesterday I started working again. Today, for the first time, the heat loses its intensity; I can feel the air getting cooler. I begin the revision of the *Journal* for 1975.

10 August

The mistral is blowing. We awake to a day of spring—a *cold* spring! I read *Manuscrit trouvé à Saragosse*. How I regret that I didn't know it the last time I talked with Roger Caillois. . . .

11 August

The mistral. Cool weather continues.

This evening, at dinner, Pierre Emmanuel and Janine. How much could be told and pondered about the friendship of Ioan Cuşa and Pierre Emmanuel! I could write a "Dialogue between Two Religious Poets."

12 August

The mistral continues, but the day is superb. Something seems to have changed—but where?

Marie-France arrives.

13 August

I work until I feel it's time for me to bathe in the pool.

This evening we visit Les Baux-de-Provence. Then dinner at the famous hotel restaurant. I should like, someday, to have one of my novella characters live in that hotel!

16 August

Yesterday and the day before, work. Every detail is as I want it, all the information is concentrated in a few pages (pondered, written, rewritten over and over); all that remains is to redact it in final form. (But I'm obsessed by the thought that this *magnum opus* might remain unfinished. . . . In which case, what would be the use of my continuing the redaction?)

This afternoon, with Ioan Cuşa and Claude-Henri Rocquet to Gordes, to visit *"le village des bories."* Extraordinary impression. One can enter, unhindered, into a village of neolithic formation, which never-theless was occupied until the seventeenth century. With just a little imagination you can discover a world of values and meanings which only with much labor can you succeed in seeing through books, pictures, and isolated artifacts in a museum.

For the first time, Ioan seemed to us rather tired.

17 August

Sometimes I wonder if I did right in abandoning *Autobiography* II in order to put the finishing touches to the pages selected for the second volume of *Fragments d'un journal.* I ought to have proceeded in the opposite direction: the *Journal* would have helped me to advance more rapidly in the writing of the *Autobiography* from 1940 on, from the time I left Romania. I have only a few notes from London and Oxford (1940–1941), but the *Portuguese Journal* is rather copious (four-hundred pages written in a small hand). Moreover, from the Parisian notebooks I have selected and published very few pages; the rest of the materials I can use in *Autobiography* II.

Among the few things I like about my "way of being" is this: my irresponsibility or indifference. I'm past seventy-two and I have two writings "on my hands" that I consider important: *Histoire* III and *Autobiography* II (if not even III!). And yet I let myself be drawn into other projects; I don't hurry—as if I had my whole life ahead of me. . . .

PARIS, 21 August

We returned this evening with Marie-France. She is happy from her week at Eygalières. We don't recognize her.

I write to Charles Smith (Macmillan and The Free Press). I know that many of my colleagues and former students will doubt the wisdom of my decision. I'm an old man, I have a great many other things to do: works in progress to finish, etc. But I said to myself that it's preferable for an encyclopedia of this kind to be planned and organized by a historian of religions rather than by a sociologist or a psychologist, or even a theologian, however competent he might be.

23 August

Two days of work, such as I haven't had in a long time. Have written almost twenty pages. (True, I've had them ready to write for several months.) Toward evening I interrupted the writing in order not to tire my right hand too much.

26 August

The day before yesterday, in the evening, Dinu Tătărescu came to pick us up. It was raining. We ate and slept at their apartment in Parly II. The next day we drove to Honfleur. The rain had stopped, but the sky was overcast. We visited Honfleur, then drove on. All those famous towns and beaches which I hadn't seen. . . . As usual, I find myself living in *another time*. Impossible to be more precise. The villas we pass remind me. . . . No, they don't *remind* me, but they "press" me more and more into that time which I can't identify. . . .

In the evening, on the highway to Paris, the rain begins again, falling harder and more stubbornly. Fortunately, I could continue my dream. . . .

27 August

This evening, dinner with Vona. We discuss, as usual, what has happened to him, what might happen, etc., etc. I listen very attentively, of course, but from time to time my mind carries me back to the beginning of our friendship, to 1949 or 1950; whenever we met then, we talked about "literature," about his novel, which, although badly translated, pleased Brice Parain, Roger Caillois, and other readers at Gallimard very much—and yet, the novel was never published. . . .

28 August

I write the preface to the Portuguese translation of the little book *Images and Symbols*. I had planned to develop certain observations about aquatic symbolism, to refer to Camoens's *Os Lusíadas,* the first "creative appearance" of the Atlantic Ocean in European literature. But being involved in many other tasks, I abandoned the idea.

30 August

Yesterday, at 5:00, meeting with Waldberg. He gives me several texts, admirably edited by himself. Plans for the future. . . .

Today, at the same hour, Nina Cassian comes to call. I had heard so much about her, both good and bad (especially bad), that I had become curious. The candor with which she criticizes herself: the foolish things (and others, more serious) which she did in the Stalinist era. She believed totally in the "historical miracle" of communism. Fortunately, she is also a musician. She composes (more interesting things all the time, she says). But she will never be able to give up poetry.

5 September

In spite of letters, I have succeeded in working—and even better than I'd expected to. But I realize that I'm still far from completing the "schedule" I had set for this vacation.

Formerly, that is, twenty or thirty years ago, the more things I had to do (to write), the better I did them, and the more quickly.

12 September

Today, a telephone call from Douglas Allen. He is in Paris for a few days. We set an hour to meet on 14 September.

Letters, letters. And yet I manage to keep working.

15 September

Unnecessary to record all the visits. This evening, invited to Paul Barbăneagră's, with friends. (The ceremonial at our leave-taking, as every fall.)

I finish the preface for Jean Servier's book, begun yesterday. The book has been out of print for a long time, and I was sorry not to be able to recommend it to certain students interested in *this way* of doing anthropology.

18 September

At 6:00 Olender comes. I am reminded of our long interview that afternoon last year when he had to conclude the session, scarcely begun, because I had just learned of the death of Henry Corbin.

19 September

A visit from Adrian Marino, among others. He is *sure* that he will be able to publish his voluminous work, *Hermeneutica lui Mircea*

Eliade, in Romania. [Translator's note: It was published in 1980 by Editura Dacia (Cluj-Napoca) and in French translation by Gallimard in 1981.]

ROTHENBURG, *22 September*

We left yesterday with Ioan and Ileana Cuşa. Lunch at Orly. By plane to Frankfurt, arriving at 5:00. Ioan had reserved a car, and a half hour later we were on the *Autobahn.* Superb trip to Rothenburg, where we arrived at nightfall. Cold. Ileana had reserved a room for us at Hotel Eisenhurt (eighteenth century)—large, superb room, like something out of a historical film. Then, our first ride around this enchanting city, the most beautiful German city I've ever seen. Too bad it's so cold. . . .

Today, in a cold autumnal rain, we visit the city. No need to record what we saw, what pleased us (in particular, the walls of the old city, the St. Jakob-Kirche, the city hall). But after an hour we take refuge in our hotel, frozen.

23 September

Ioan's weakness concerns me. He scarcely touches his plates of food, although, it would seem, he chose them with much eagerness. I catch him taking aspirin frequently; rheumatic pains, he says. He explains his lack of appetite in this way: after his operation of a year ago, his whole digestive system shrank.

PARIS, *26 September*

Another half day lost with correspondence and visits. I open the journal of Emerson and find these lines, which fascinate me: "What a pity that we cannot curse and swear in good society! Cannot the stinging dialect of the sailors be domesticated? It is the best rhetoric, and for a hundred occasions those forbidden words are the only good ones" (October 24, 1840). Obviously, things have long since changed, but not, I fear, in the sense Emerson would have wanted.

29 September

At 4:00 I go to see Georges Dumézil. I don't understand the melancholy that came over me as soon as we sat down at the table in the living room. G. D. seems to me as lucid, energetic, and creative as ever. He talks about his work: it's as though I'm listening to a young *normalien* summarizing his doctoral thesis.

CHICAGO, *2 October*

We left Paris yesterday morning. Ioana and Costin Mireanu took us to the airport. We took off an hour late (the Boston airport was closed on account of the visit of the pope). At Boston we changed planes, but we waited two more hours. We landed at O'Hare at 7:30; a horrible flight; thunderstorms. It was after 10:00 when we reached home, exhausted (it was morning in Paris).

Today, although tired, we dined at the home of the French consul general, G. Fieschi, in order to meet the French ambassador, M. François de Laboulaye.

3 October

Extraordinarily tired—more so than ever before after returning form Europe. I spend a good part of the afternoon in bed, sleeping. Christinel goes to the inauguration of our institute (the Institute for Advanced Religious Research); it was for this ceremony, in which the university president, Hanna Gray, is also participating, that we returned early to Chicago!

Nevertheless, I put in an appearance at the dinner in the Quadrangle Club. I shake the president's hand. But I skip the lecture held at 8:00 P.M.

5 October

I believe I'm beginning to feel better. But I am "detached" from Chicago (why?). It's as if this were to be my last year of teaching here. I write to Corina; then to Ion Lotreanu and Virgil Nemoianu.

7 October

I write to my translator into Dutch, Lisbeth des Plantes, and to Ioan Cuşa, asking him to send her a copy of *Noaptea de Sânziene* [The Forbidden Forest].

10 October

This evening, from 7:30 to 10:00, seminar with Wendy: "Religious Symbolism in Historical Context." I succeed in speaking rather well, but I lack the *enthusiasm* of other times.

11 October

I observe that I can no longer recognize faces at three or four yards' distance. At the same time, the fingers of both hands (but especially the right) are stiff (gout?) from one morning to the next; I kill the pain with eight Bufferin tablets (''arthritis strength'') per day, but I write with difficulty and often cannot hold a pen in my hand.

And the mysterious fatigue continues. I'm exhausted after taking a few steps through the room. At the office I go about very slowly, like an old man just out of the hospital.

15 October

Charles Smith, vice-president of Macmillan Publishing Company, comes from New York City to see me. He had written to me already at Paris, and he telephoned me last week. We talk for almost two hours. He insists that I accept the general direction of the new *Encyclopedia of Religion* (in sixteen volumes!) which they have in mind to publish. I would be editor in chief, I would have a board of editors chosen by myself, and I would decide on the general lines, the method, and the contributors.

I accept.

23 October

I'm going to stop recording here the names of persons I meet with and those to whom I improvise letters almost daily. I hope I'll be careful to set them down in the *Datebook*.

24 October

For a week my hands, especially my *fingers*, have been stiff. The gout, which the Parisian woman doctor cured two years ago.

So: the eyes (cataract), the "head" (I seem unable to work "seriously"), and the hand (I write with great difficulty). All at one time.

30 October
Superb day. In the evening David Tracy takes us to the circus. I haven't seen a circus in I don't know how many years. As usual, fascinated. But, no matter how close I pushed the glasses toward my eyes, I couldn't see anything but the camels, elephants, and horses. (And the doctor assures me he cannot prescribe thicker lenses. . . .)

When we return, we eat dinner at the Medici Cafeteria on Fifty-seventh Street. The middle of the night, and we could hardly find a place to sit. But the students didn't seem too numerous.

5 November
I finish transcribing the *Journal* for the year 1977.

A few days ago, a discussion about the book *Life after Life* by Raymond A. Moody. I said to the others: what seems interesting to me in the examples cited by the author is not their potential value as "documents" illustrating the survival of souls, but their *scenario*. Why do the same motifs recur so many times: the bridge, the blinding light, the beautiful landscape, etc.? Let us admit, from the outset, that the soul does not "survive." It is a matter, then, of a no less enigmatic phenomenon: before passing into infinity, the man witnesses the unfolding of a dramatic, complex, and fascinating scenario. Why? One could say that Life (i.e., material life) reveals again, for the last time, its beauty and meaning. But *why?*

13–17 November
At Billings Hospital. Since the first day, four doctors have examined me. The second and third days, all sorts of tests (blood, sputum, etc.) and X rays. Dr. Cohen suggested I enter the hospital because the tests made in the last several weeks showed me to be slightly anemic, and he wanted to identify the cause. They found an iron deficiency. But there were other problems too: spots on the lungs, which have grown larger since the last time I was X-rayed (the rheumatologist believes that

it may be connected with the arthritis, another doctor believes there are traces of tuberculosis from youth and that there is possibly a recurrence of the disease). After the stomach X-ray, there is no longer any doubt: an ulcer, probably provoked by an excess of aspirin (six to eight pills a day, for six or seven weeks). Therefore, doctor's orders: no coffee, no alcohol, no aspirin—and a great many antacids, iron supplements, etc.

The thing that annoys me the most: I can't take aspirin (actually Bufferin) any more when I suffer acute arthritic pains. Just very hot baths. (Yesterday I held my hands in a container of hot paraffin. Wonderful sensation—no pain, the first time in almost two months!)

And yet, the fatigue. Can it be only the effect of the ulcer? They told me it's not bleeding too badly.

18 November

Extraordinarily beautiful day! "Indian summer." I begin the novella *Dayan*. I write twelve pages.

19 November

Rain. I write eight pages. But tomorrow, Wednesday, 20 November, we're leaving for New York, and I don't know if I'll be able to continue the novella.

NEW YORK, 20–25 November

I tried to write; had to give it up after two hours of futile effort. Have reread *The Pursuit of the Millennium* by Norman Cohen and begun Bernard McGinn's *Visions of the End,* an excellent anthology of medieval apocalyptic texts.

Lisette invited some fourteen friends for Thanksgiving. I was not at all "in form": I spent a good part of the evening in our room, reading. The arthritic pains in the hands continue.

I went to Ruth Nanda Anshen's place to discuss the text I shall write for the Threshold Foundation.

CHICAGO, 27 November

With great effort—because my hands are so stiff—I begin the chapter on the Balto-Slavs. Fortunately, I found the whole file with text and summaries prepared for a course in the fall of 1960 (!), which, however, I did not teach; the students requested me then to speak about Egyptian and Mesopotamian religions instead.

I found also materials collected in a folder which I had placed long ago inside the voluminous monograph of Evel Gasparini, *Il Matriarcho Slavo*—a folder I lost track of several years ago.

28 November

At Billings, to see Dr. Cohen. He tells me that the ulcer is duodenal—the kind I had ten or eleven years ago. I must continue the regimen and treatment until Christmas.

He gives me nothing for the arthritis.

29 November

Yesterday evening and this evening, the seminar. I worked a little—badly—on the Balto-Slavic chapter.

[*Datebook*

23–26 December, New York: Juliana and Roger come to see us, with their baby. I try in vain to work (the chapter about the Altaics).]

PALM BEACH, *26 December*

Superb weather. We arrive at 5:00. Staying at the Ocean Echo. Two connecting rooms, with baths. Lydia M. is waiting for us at the airport. At 9:30 she goes again, with Christinel, to meet Lisette.

27 December–2 January

Superb weather the whole time. On 30 December, I take up *Dayan* again. I write some twenty pages. Lunch at the Beach Club. 31 December at Lydia's. I write. We telephoned Corina on 28 December.

1 January 1980

I write all day. Dinner at Lydia's in the evening.

2 January

Short letters: Corina, Goma, C. Grigorescu, Tănase.

This evening at the airport, a surprise: our plane had left at 2:10 (Christinel thought it was at 21:00). Some anxious moments. Finally, we find two seats on another flight. It is past midnight when we arrive in Chicago.

CHICAGO, *5 January*

It's snowing and cold. Christinel has a cold; she regrets it especially because she couldn't go to the dinner prepared by Anthony and Priscilla in honor of Nathan Scott.

Since yesterday, I'm writing with fervor at *Dayan*. It's been a long time since I've known such euphoria.

6 January

Have I recorded anywhere this statement of Cecil B. deMille: "I want a story that begins with an earthquake and works up to a climax"?

8 January

In the last two days I have continued the novella with the same enthusiasm. I've written and transcribed some eighty-one pages so far. With a little luck, I could finish *Dayan* in a few more days. If only I didn't have so many letters to answer!

9 January

Thirty years since our marriage. The sky is clearer than ever, but the cold continues and a strong wind has begun to blow.

I send Christinel a "romantic bouquet" of bird of paradise flowers. The seminar on the history of religions will begin this evening, but Wendy will conduct it alone. We shall dine at the Kitagawas'. They have announced some surprises: champagne and "other symbolic souvenirs." Moreover, it will be Christinel's first time out since our return from Palm Beach.

12 January

Each day I've written ten to fifteen pages, and today I finished *Dayan*. Too tired to transcribe the ending—although I'm eager for Christinel to read it.

14 January

Yesterday I corrected and transcribed the last pages. Christinel is enthusiastic—although she wonders how many readers will understand the ending. I reply, jokingly: "Either all, or none!"

18 January

In the last five days I've been almost completely occupied with writing letters and making up packets of books (the majority, recent translations of my works). Sometimes I wonder why I *consent* to such drudgery.

14 March

I receive M. Handoca's book, *Mircea Eliade: Contribuţii biobibliografice*. The first book about me to appear in the Romanian Socialist Republic. A telegram of a few days ago informed me of the appearance of Handoca's volume.

15 March

Jean Gouillard sends me a copy of *Le Temps* of 9 March 1907 (!)—with these lines: *"Le 'temps profane' retrouvé!"* [profane time rediscovered].

26 March

Today I receive the book by A. Marino, *Hermeneutica lui Mircea Eliade*.

31 March

All last week spent in: (1) transcribing some thirty pages of my *Journal* from Yucatán and Guatemala (December 1978) and (2) selecting books for Meadville (almost sixty volumes) and for "students" (over a hundred books and pamphlets, which will be sold by L. Sullivan and the proceeds given to the students).

I still have to finish the transcription of the *Journal* and to make a catalogue of the books I want to send to Corina in Bucharest, to replace, at least in part, those fifteen hundred volumes she lost in 1943–1944. Then, with God's help, I'll begin the classifying of my files and manuscripts.

28 April

I've decided to give up the presidency of the International Association for the History of Religions, which I accepted at the urging of Zwi Werblowsky in the spring of 1978. Too many troubles, too much politics, etc. Also, I shall cancel the public lecture announced for the congress in August at Winnipeg.

June

I wonder if I did right to publish the first volume of my memoirs *now*. I've reread only a few chapters, but I'm afraid my exaggerated "candor" and "modesty" minimalize a certain conduct (from earliest youth) which was not lacking in *grandeur* and nobility.

PARIS, 5 July

A month since we arrived. Except for the first few days, it has rained all the time. An overcast, gray, leaden sky—like November. Depressed, with no desire to work; I feel the need of light, of the sun, as plants do. The cold weather in the middle of summer doesn't bother me, but the darkness, which has lasted for three weeks, makes me ill.

16 July

Inexplicably, my inhibition continues: for a week, ever since I reread the material brought from Chicago about Tibetan religions, I've been trying in vain to start writing the chapter. I wonder if this atony has a deeper meaning: is it trying to tell me that I *must* give up *Histoire* III and devote my last years of activity to the completion of the *Autobiography?*

21 July

The first sunny day. Blue sky, with a few white, lazy clouds. I go to the Jardin des Plantes, which I hadn't entered in several years. I arrive at noon and stroll leisurely, without thoughts, for better than an hour. The Museum of Natural Sciences is closed for repairs, but I hear about an exposition of *"les plus beaux insectes"* nearby, at 45 rue Buffon. Only one large room, but how impressive! I linger till 2:00. Thrilled to discover that enormous coleopteron, green with two gold spots on the elytrums, like the one I saw, dead, in the hand of a child in Darjeeling in 1929. I record its name here: *Megaloxantna bicolor gigantea.* I bought it, then, for six annas and brought it to Calcutta, to Ripon Street. Don't remember now to whom I gave it.

A superb, enormous blue butterfly from Guinea is named *Papilio zalmoxis* (Hewiton). I wonder why I visit the gigantic greenhouse with those tropical trees growing thirty-five to forty feet high amidst the vines, and the gallery of cacti, and that stifling room in which I feel my breathing become labored and I start to perspire. . . .

The last two hours at the Ménagerie. Early memories of the Paris of 1947–1948. As usual, the four or five bears beg, standing on their hind legs with open mouths—and skillfully catch the peanuts thrown them by the visitors.

EYGALIÈRES, *9 August*

Here five days. The weather continues as pleasant as ever. Distressed at how I found Ioan.

12 August

I reread the poems of Eminescu in P. P. Panaitescu's edition. Continually interrupted by visitors.

CHICAGO, *October*

Sanda Loga, who went to Romania this summer to visit her parents, heard a throng of peasants from Maramureş in a procession at the Agapia monastery singing:

> We pray to thee, Mary,
> To help us constantly
> To believe always
> That God exists.

29 November

Am making a great effort to write these few lines *legibly*. For the past two months, writing's been a torture. That's why, when I'm forced to take a few notes or write a page or two, I content myself with signs and abbreviations. Unfortunately, after a few days those signs become undecipherable. . . .

On 18 October I began the treatment recommended by Dr. Sorensen. The results are modest. For example, the fingers and joints seem more fragile than before. On 15 December we will make an attack on a "second front," as Dr. Sorensen says, with the gold treatment.

I suffer especially because I can't write, can't take notes, can't answer letters except with a ridiculous effort (for one letter of two pages I work about as long as I ought to write a review or a short article).

11 January 1981

With great conviction, André Gide reflects the whole "ideology" he hated in his youth: "Nous commençons à entrevoir la fin de l'époque mythologique" (*Journal*, 25 October 1927). [We are beginning to glimpse the end of the mythological era.] Or this: " 'Mais qu'entendez-vous par mystique?' 'Ce qui pré-suppose et exige l'abdication de la raison' " (*Journal*, 9 November 1927). ["But what do you mean by mysticism?" "That' which presupposes and requires the abdication of reason."]

20 January

Padmasambhava prophesied the vogue of Buddhism and the Tibetans in America: "When the iron bird flies and horses run on wheels, the Tibetan people will be scattered like ants across the world and the Dharma will come to the land of the Red Man."

22 January

Yesterday evening, the first seminar, "Myths of the Origin of Death." What an exciting subject! . . . It ought to constitute a chapter of the book I've been preparing for a long time, *Mythologies of Death*. But before I finish *Histoire des idées religieuses*, I don't dare begin it.

Today, at Billings Hospital, the first injection with colloidal gold. Dr. Sorensen told me that the treatment will go on for a long time: the effects of the gold will be felt only after ten or twelve shots. . . .

27 January

The second injection. At five o'clock. I feel bad: vertigo, fatigue. Is this, perhaps, a reaction to the gold salts? If I can't stand it, the treatment will have to be changed.

28 January

The vertigo and weakness continue. I can't hold the seminar.

30 January

This evening, with Alexandra and Saul Bellow, Sanda L., and Chris Gamwell at the Italian Village Restaurant.

I receive the first copies of *Uniformes de général* and the new edition of *Images et symboles* (in the series *Idées*), with the preface by Georges Dumézil. (Twenty years after its appearance, this little book continues to be reprinted—although it doesn't compare with the other "popular" books, such as *Traité, Le Yoga, Le Mythe de l'éternel retour,* etc.).

I continue, fascinated, with Dostoevski's *Les Démons*, ten or twenty pages every night. But I break off the reading before 1:00; otherwise, I'd stay at it all night, as in the old days.

2 February

Am preparing the plan for the articles in section B (Institutions, Rituals, Religious Concepts, etc.) for the *Encyclopedia*. At the same time, I'm trying to find the most suitable contributors; I'm thinking, especially, of European scholars.

Very cold, like yesterday.

3 February

The cold weather continues: $-3°F$. I work at the list of subjects (for each article I have to write several lines, indicating to the author the context in which he must write).

This evening, the dizziness returns.

4 February

Although I am still dizzy, I hold the seminar. It's curious that the vertigo attacks don't prevent me from saying interesting things. . . .

5 February

Dizzy at lunchtime.

I finish the list of subjects for the *Encyclopedia,* section B (it's not exhaustive, of course).

6 February

This evening, at the Quadrangle Club with Henry Fraize, from French Television. He proposes to me again—although I refused him the first time, when he telephoned from New York—that I prepare and direct a series of four or five programs (each an hour in length!) about the universal history of religions, beginning with "primitives" (the television team would film in Australia, Africa, and South America), presenting the great Asian religions (they would go to India, China, Barabudur—anywhere I say), concluding with the biblical religions.

I confess to him that I'm incapable of thinking or speaking in front of cameras.

10 February

Ordinarily I don't read many articles about myself (especially those published in Romania in recent years), but in the ones I have read, I've never seen anyone bringing out this fact: that I am an author *without a model.* I resemble, or want to resemble, Hasdeu, Cantemir, and Goethe. But look very closely at our writings and ideas, our beliefs and *lives*: which of my great predecessors, indeed, has constituted for me a model? Their example gave me courage, that's all.

20 *February*

I transcribe here several phrases or sentences from *Les Démons* (Editions Pléiade), which I set down while reading it. The only way of being able to reread them later:

" 'L'athéisme russe s'est toujours contenté de calembours,' grogne Chatov" (151). ["Russian atheism always contents itself with puns," growled Shatov.]

"Il y a des gens chez lesquels le linge propre est presqu'une inconvenance,' avait répondu Lipoutine" (150). ["They are people with whom clean linen is almost an impropriety," Lipoutin had answered.]

Lébiadkine to Varvara Pétrovna: "Madame, selon moi la Russie n'est qu'un jeu de la nature, rien de plus" (186). ["According to me, Russia is just a game of Nature, nothing more."]

" 'Un athée se souvient d'être un Russe.' 'Celui qui devient athée cesse immédiatement d'être Russe' " (Stavroguine, 267). ["An atheist remembers to be a Russian." "One who becomes an atheist ceases immediately to be a Russian."]

"Pour faire un civet il faut un lièvre, pour croire en Dieu il faut un Dieu" (Stavroguine, 267). ["To make a rabbit stew, you must have a rabbit; to believe in God, you must have a God."]

"Lorsque je servais encore dans les hussards, il m'arrivait souvent de songer à Dieu" (Major Maximovitch, 420). ["When I was still serving in the Hussars, it often came to me to think of God."]

2 *March*

Hinduism, Buddhism, Christianity, Islam—all assimilated local cults and divinities, according to the well-known system. By this means, through a process of integration into a major religious tradition, there were preserved a great many marginal, provincial beliefs and conceptions otherwise condemned, with time, to fossilization and disappearance.

But this process was already operating centuries earliér. Zeus assimilated numerous divinities of the sky and storm. And in Vedic and Brahmanic India, the assimilation of aboriginal gods, their blending into the *archetypes* of Hinduism, is a process still going on today. These innumerable and continuous assimilations *solidify the structure* of the deity, reconfirming his/her universality.

8 March

Gide, about Freud: "Mais que de choses absurdes chez cet imbécile de génie!" (*Journal,* 19 June 1924). [But what absurd things in the work of that imbecile of a genius!]

15 March

As one of my characters in the novella *Podul* (The bridge) says: "All sorts of things happen." Scarcely had I met him when John W., that young theological student (very gifted, they say), confessed to me that, in the seminars, he couldn't forget those two propositions from the *Confessions* of St. Augustine: *Sero te amavi* (I came to love Thee late) and *Iam te amabam* (I loved Thee long ago). It seemed to him that they constitute the *true* key to Augustinian theology. He dared to consult one of his professors, who smiled and patted him on the shoulder in a fatherly way. But he was not discouraged, and he continued to meditate on the hidden meaning of those two propositions. "I've spent several years at it," he added melancholically.

21 March

Bruce Lincoln, a former student of mine, today a professor in Missouri, invited us to the House of Hunan. His wife was with him, and he wanted at all costs for us to dine together. Bruce is one of the most gifted of my former students, and I am proud of him, even venturing to brag about him. Like Ioan Culianu, he knows many languages and is concerned with diverse and "interesting" problems. He writes not only about Indo-European matters, but also about "primitives." And he is "productive": dozens of articles, two books published and two others in preparation.

But he says to me very frankly that I made a big mistake in accepting, *at my age,* the responsibility of editor in chief of the *Encyclopedia.* (He's right, of course, but my "sacrifice" has a deep meaning.)

4 April

I invite Siegfried Unseld to Maxim's (Christinel still has a cold). Long discussion. Siegfried shows me the plan for the ten volumes of my *Werke*. He speaks to me about Dr. Ludwig, to whom he has entrusted the editing of this edition.

NEW YORK, *15–20 April*

For the first time, we see two stage plays (we've had the tickets for a whole month): *Amadeus* on April 16 and, the following evening, *Edith Piaf.*

Visited Arthur Cohen on the eighteenth. We dined the next day at Tantzi and Brutus Coste's.

CHICAGO, *23–26 April*

Work session for the *Encyclopedia,* with Conyers, Charles Adams, Victor Turner, and others.

Final session today, April 26. Dinner at the Kitagawas' tonight.

1 May

Victor Turner told me this about Raymond Firth: At about age 77 or 78, having been invited to hold a series of lectures at some university (since his retirement he had been living quietly on his small property in his homeland), everyone surrounded him and congratulated him on his excellent physical condition. After a while these comments began to annoy him. "Yes," said Firth, "I do feel rather well, but my father's not in very good health." Indeed, a few months later the old gentleman died, in Australia, at the age of 104!

6 May

I copy this sentence from Fontenelle (for Emil Cioran's benefit, especially!): "Plus on a d'années, plus on voit de quelle importance il serait de n'avoir pas tant!" [The more years one has, the more he sees how important it would be not to have so many!]

9 May

Many vice-presidents of the United States have been forgotten. Thomas R. Marshall, for example, is known only for having said: "What this country needs is a good five-cent cigar."

22 May

Telephone call from François Cochet, Ioan Cuşa's associate. Ileana asked him to tell us about Ioan's death. . . . And how confident we were that we would find him alive! Too upset to write more.

1 June

Yesterday I met Hans Peter Duerr, German anthropologist and philosopher, who is preparing a *Festschrift* for me of one-thousand pages. It will appear in two or three volumes in September 1982, at Suhrkamp Verlag, Frankfurt. He will, of course, reproduce in German translation several articles already published. But there will be many new contributions, a number of them (he added, smiling) rather "critical." As he explains: he wants to present a *total view* of my works, both literary and scientific.

A likeable young man, with hair (rather thin) hanging to his shoulders, dressed like a student, without a necktie. We dine at the Quadrangle Club with the Kitagawas (Joe brought a tie for him; otherwise he wouldn't have been admitted to the dining room). Then, at our place, till midnight.

3 June

In the past several months I've written less and less in the *Journal* (and I've even neglected the *Datebook*). I write with great effort. And especially—I'm tired, sleepy, "detached." (Can this be the effects of the colloidal gold treatments?)

At the end of April I finished, with a mighty effort, chapter 33 of *Histoire*. Since then I've continued to read and take notes, but haven't redacted anything.

4 June

Preparations for leaving. First to New York on 9 June; then to Paris.

Exceptionally tired all the time. And yet I can't believe that I'm an *uomo finito!* (People all around me tell me it's the effects of the injections of gold salts.)

6 June

I begin to understand Y., who confessed last winter that he no longer dared to read Nietzsche: he prophesied and anticipated too precisely all that has happened in the West for almost a century! In an article I was leafing through absent-mindedly, I chanced upon this sentence: "La démocratisation de l'Europe nous prépare, trés involontairement, uns pépiniêre de tyrans." [The democratization of Europe is preparing for us, quite involuntarily, a seedbed for tyrants.]

PARIS, 5 July

After forty-one years, I see Cella Delavrancea again. (I believe I saw her last at the funeral of Nae Ionescu, in March of 1940, a few weeks before I left for London.) I went to get her in a taxi, which I had engaged so we could arrive in time at Chez Carlos, where Christinel was waiting for us.

To me she seemed unchanged, although she is now ninety-four. She practices the piano here at Paris for three or four hours per day. She recalls a great many events from her youth. I don't believe, however, that she is "up to date," as they say, with what has happened in the last ten or fifteen years. She tells me that she came to Paris this time (she's staying at an apartment put at her disposal by a French friend) *in order to eat.* In Romania, even with the money she has to spend, she finds almost nothing.

We have lunch, then go to our place. Our conversation lasts until almost 6:00. Christinel and I feel rather tired, but not Cella! In the cab, on the way back to her apartment, she continues to talk.

What should I note first? At Iaşi, in 1917, after the signing of the armistice, [between Romania and the Axis], Barbu Delavrancea takes to his bed. The doctors find nothing wrong. Barbu Delavrancea simply doesn't want to live, *can't* live any more. To his daughters he says one day: "We knew we were entering the war unprepared, but we knew that it was the last moment when, by entering it, we could obtain from the Allies the assurance of the reintegration of the country! For the time being, the contest is lost. I know it's not final, but *I* can't go on living. May you live, and may you be happy!" A few days afterward, he died.

She didn't say anything about Nae Ionescu. (Probably those splendid letters which Nae sent her in the winter of 1939 from the military hospital at Braşov have been lost. Maybe she destroyed them herself during the time of Stalinism.)

7 July

What Cella Delavrancea told me about King Carol I: In the summer of 1915, at Peleş, he asked her a question, but accompanied it with a smile such as Cella had never seen before. She was petrified and couldn't reply. A few days later, King Carol died.

On the front in Moldavia in 1916–1917, whenever she saw that same smile on the lips of a wounded man, she knew that he would soon die.

Cella about Christinel: She is like a clear lake in which some poplar trees are reflected.

July

I finish reading the journal which Ioan Cuşa kept in the last months before his death (January-May). His extraordinary willpower, to record several times per day (sometimes after midnight) all the symptoms, pains, and results of the treatments, specifying the dosage and the hour at which he took such and such medicine, his reactions (positive or negative) and their duration, etc. He states in one place that these notes could "serve later" (whom?—Dr. Bloncourt, of course, but perhaps also himself, because for a long time Ioan believed he'd be cured; he was convinced it was a case of cirrhosis).

No less precious and moving are the recollections from his Dobrogean childhood (I suggested to Ileana that they be published; Christinel will type them). And others—from the Siberian prison camp, from the student years, from the first years spent in France. There are, in addition, judgments about friends and political events, etc. Unfortunately, they can't be published until later.

Ioan Cuşa wrote in his journal on 16 May 1980: "I do exactly as our old crones: I do not shrink from death, but face it."

23 July

Corina arrives. She seems younger and in better health than she was two years ago. This time, three employees of the Romania Association, sent by V. C., accompanied her to the airport to simplify matters at customs. She brought me several things, including the Russian silver icon beneath which our parents' votive candle burned in their bedroom. Thus, she didn't have to undergo the stress of the other time, which exhausted her. (If I were to accept the invitation to visit the country, what a life Corina would live, and how much simpler Sorin's life would be!)

I see the first copy of E. Simion's edition of my fantastic novellas [*În curte la dionis,* Bucharest: Cartea Românească, 1981]. Sixty thousand copies printed, but only 30,100 have been released now; the rest, in the fall. Bad paper, gray ink. The book is priced at twenty-seven lei, but it can't be found; the bookstores sold it under the counter. On the black market, Corina tells me, a copy goes for three hundred lei.

My only satisfaction: this volume includes *Pe strada Mântuleasa* and *Les Trois Grâces.* But I don't have the time—or the curiosity—to check to see if they have respected the original text.

EYGALIÈRES, *4 August*

We arrived last evening. As she did last year, Ileana came to take us, by car, from Avignon. The presence of Corina probably enabled her to keep her emotions under control.

Troubled, and yet fascinated, we rediscover this magnificent villa, which Ioan built, very largely, with his own hands. This morning the sky is like crystal. Warm, but with a gentle breeze. As before, we walk on the grass under the trees to the back of the orchard, where we find the last lamb left from the flock of past years.

6 August

The weather continues as magnificent as at first. I bathed in the swimming pool (physiotherapy!). But my hands—the finger joints—are very stiff. I write with difficulty. For the time being, I'm doing nothing; I tell myself I have to rest (although for many months I haven't made any great effort).

We dine at the restaurant in Baux, guests of Dr. Bloncourt and Marie-Claude. Ileana brought us an hour early so Corina could see the ruins of that fortress-castle destroyed by Richelieu in 1633. We revisit the melancholy Church of St. Vincent (twelfth or thirteenth century); and once more, I regret not having attended the midnight services celebrated for the shepherds of the region.

8 August

I spend a good part of the day in the "tower" built by Ioan, almost single-handedly, for his library, sitting at the long, hard, superb table, seemingly made to induce you to write. I have reread G. Scholem's *Les origins de la Kabbale* for paragraphs still not written in the chapter on Jewish mysticism. I take notes with difficulty; each line demands time and patience; my fingers are quite as contracted as they were last winter.

14 August

Today Rodica, Marie-France, and Eugène Ionesco left, after a six-day stay. Long discussions. But to me Eugène seemed depressed, "anguished"—and he himself repeats several times a day that he is so lacking in desire to work that he can't read anything but newspapers.

A month ago, when we spent two days at his "Mill" (13–15 July), he was better. I try to console him as best I can (actually, I tell him, it's a cyclothymia, like many others, etc.).

17 August

Of all the many "spectacular gestures" of Dr. Bloncourt (spectacular for others, not for him), I want to record this one:

A young Breton, condemned by the doctors, confesses to him (some ten days before he died) how happy he would be if he could see his family and village in Brittany once again. Dr. B. assures him that his wish will be granted. Together with Marie-Claude, the doctor removes all that can be removed from his four-seat airplane in order to make room for the patient—and a few hours later they land in the vicinity of his natal village. In this way the young man could say good-bye to all his people.

The doctor scarcely knew him; the young man was not, properly speaking, his patient. (Note: Bloncourt declares himself to be an atheist.)

ROME, *3 September*

We arrive at 2:30. Horia Roman is waiting for us at the airport. I am glad to find him unchanged. We have rooms reserved at Hotel Plaza, on Via del Corso Veneto. Our room has a window overlooking an internal garden, full of flowers.

We invite to dinner at the Capriciosa: Mrs. Adamiu, Nina Batalli, Horia, and Mrs. Barbu Brezianu.

Corina is seeing Rome again after exactly fifty years. She toured Italy, from Abbazia to Palermo, on her honeymoon.

4 September

I am depressed by, among other things, the shoving, loudness, and aggressive behavior of a few young couples, especially on Via Veneto. But I recovered peace and solitude once I arrived at the monument of Augustus; and on the banks of the Tiber only a few tourists are strolling, disoriented.

5 September

This afternoon Al. Caprariu comes to see me. He is staying at the *pension* of Mrs. Petraşincu; he's in Italy for a month or so, invited by C. Dragan. He tells me about many happenings in the homeland.

This evening we dine with Yvonne Rossignon at Nina and Nicola Ciarletta's. As usual, long discussion with Nicola.

At 6:00 Gherardo Gnoli, successor to Tucci as the director of the Oriental Institute, comes to see me. We talk till 8:00. I find out many things about the situation of our discipline (the history of religions, Oriental studies) in Italy. I invite him to write the article on Iranian religions for the *Encyclopedia*. Tucci is ill, but Gnoli will telephone him and hopes we can see him together.

At 8:30, invited by the Oriental Institute (ISMEO) to the restaurant Mario (Via delle Vite). Present also are Mario Bussagli and L. Lanciotto (whom I had not seen in many years), the Sanskritist Rahiaro Gnoli, and a young Indianist, Scialbi. Enthusiastic discussion until 11:00. I feel "stimulated," indefatigable, optimistic (concerning my works in the course of elaboration), as in olden times . . . .

6 September

I spend a good share of the afternoon at the Etruscan Museum in Villa Giulia. I take several notes in a pocket notebook. But I wonder now if I'll be able to decipher them later. I ought to transcribe and develop them right away.

Then, to San Pietro, in order to meet Christinel and Corina. I try not to remember about the long visits I made in my youth. Impossible; I keep returning, in spite of myself, to that morning in 1927 when . . . .

Invited by Mrs. Adamiu, we dine in a picturesque restaurant beside Piazza Navona. After dinner we set out on foot for our hotel. We can hardly believe our eyes: the famous piazza is unrecognizable. Half-filled with hippies, drug addicts, and adventurers. (Mrs. Adamiu tells us that drugs worth a billion lire are sold here daily.)

Fortunately, as soon as we emerged from the Piazza Navona we entered that superb medieval Rome in which I resided for some nine weeks in the spring of 1928 (on Via della Scrofa, no. 3, if I remember correctly). It seems to have remained the same. Melancholy, fascination.

This long walk at night has reconciled me with Rome. I no longer regret having come.

7 September

At 3:30, Gnoli and Scialbi come to take me in the car belonging to the Oriental Institute. After leaving Tivoli, we begin to ascend. The village S. Paolo dei Cavalieri is located on top of the hill, at an altitude of some two-thousand feet. We feel we are in the mountains. ("Here, winter has already begun," Francesca Bonardi, Tucci's companion for over twenty-five years, will say). A huge house, four stories high, with terraces or walls of glass on all sides. And a terraced garden that descends for several hundred yards . . . .

We find Giuseppe Tucci in bed, dressed, covered with a blanket. The accident of five months ago: he broke his femur and was operated on unskillfully. Not only can he not walk with a cane, but I had the impression that he can't move himself in the bed. Signora Francesca turns him. Probably he suffers from other ailments, because his face is pale, with great red spots.

He speaks clearly, intelligently, with humor, but sometimes he hesitates, seeking the right word. I remind him of our first meeting: in January 1929, in the home of Dasgupta, 1404 Bakulbagon Road. He retains even now a great admiration for Dasgupta. Then he talks about his *magnum opus,* which he hopes to be able to finish: *Eros and Thanatos in Indian Thought.* (But Gnoli told me that Tucci has no desire to dictate, and his handwriting has always been indecipherable. Only two persons at ISMEO are able to decipher it.) I listen to him also, with mounting melancholy, planning an international congress on Euroasiatic civilization, at which he wants me to participate no matter what (he regrets that I won't be able to attend the congress in Venice in November, on the cultures of Central Asia!).

Signora Francesca brings soft drinks and whiskey. I content myself with a glass of mineral water. Tucci asks for a little Scotch, which he drinks straight, without ice. "To lower the tension," he says. Several cats are running in and out, under the bed and over the couch. Tucci is violently critical of the age in which we are living. He is sure that the end (somehow apocalyptic) is near. But he is not despondent: "The light" (i.e., the Spirit) will remain, whatever may happen.

He interests himself in the activity of the institute, the archeological expeditions, books, the journal *East and West.* Moreover, Gnoli visits him at least once a month, in order to keep him up to date. I realize once

again that Tucci is the only Italian savant who has created a "school."
(What has become, for example, of the "school" of Pettazzoni, in
whom I once believed?)

After an hour, as I was leaving, we kissed each other on both cheeks.
I was overwhelmed by the impression that this was our last meeting.
Fortunately, Signora Francesca invited me to tour the house; full of
"antiquities" and art objects (but the true "treasures" are kept at the
bank: "We hope that they're still there!" added Signora Francesca).

8 September

At 3:00 Mario Bussagli comes to call, together with his son,
about twenty-four who is a painter. A great admirer of mine, Bussagli
had told me earlier. The young man repeats, timidly, that the reading of
my books—in particular, *Forgerons et alchimistes,*—"enlightened"
him; his painting is dominated by the symbolism of alchemy. He shows
me several works: admirable, original, some truly fascinating. Am
surprised and gratified to learn that at his first exhibition they were
successful, both with the public and the critics.

Bussagli returns to the "cardinal" importance of the first two volumes
of *Histoire*. (He had spoken to me about them at the dinner Saturday
evening.) The chapters about Iranian religions seem to him "sensational." (Listening to him, I thought about the destiny of this work: I have
such difficulties writing—it tires me and depresses me—that I wonder
if I'll ever succeed in finishing it as I had envisioned it, if I'll be forced
to limit myself to the first part of the third volume . . . .)

At 4:00 Dan Petraşincu comes. He seems unchanged after fifteen
years. He's seventy-one and looks fifty or fifty-five. He will be leaving
soon, for the tenth time, for India. And he has been everywhere: on
UNESCO missions, to international conferences, with scholarships for
study, as a newspaperman, etc. Enthusiastic about India, the Orient—
and he repeats that he learned much from my books and my example.
I'm glad to meet a Romanian writer who has *succeeded* in realizing his
dream. He confesses to me frankly that he has two cars and plenty of
money—because of the help of a rich lady-friend.

He shows me questions for a possible interview. I promise to answer him from Chicago.

9 September

Last evening, at 6:00, Camilian Demetrescu came with his wife. He showed me photos of several of his works which he will exhibit this fall. I was too tired (I had begun "the dialogues" with Dr. Sebastian Petrescu at 2:00) to explain to him, as I wanted, certain meanings in *Nouăsprezece trandafiri*. He was enthusiastic about the book. He believes it "carries an important message" for contemporaries: how we can save ourselves in a desacralized and imbecilized world. He asks me if I have *said everything* in this book. What "technique" could help us to obtain the saving *anamnesis?* Etc., etc.

Dinner at Nina and Nicola Ciarletta's place. Present also was the widow of Professor Onciulescu, of whose death we had heard recently.

PARIS, *11 September*

We returned yesterday. The weather is as beautiful as it was at Rome. I write to Horia Stamatu about Marcel Avramescu and alchemy.

I lost my reading glasses on the plane. Urgent visit to the ophthalmologist.

20 September

For several days, depressed; seemingly struggling with an asthenia which I do not succeed in overcoming until toward evening. Am haunted by the image of Tucci in bed, covered with a blanket—he who hiked thousands of miles from one end of the Himalayas to the other. I'm thinking too of the precipitous and fatal degradation of the globe: in fifty years the quantity of carbon dioxide will transform the planet into a "hothouse." But why go on?

Chicago, 8 October

We arrive this evening. Fortunately, the driver agrees (for a reward) to carry our luggage upstairs (I can do almost nothing with my hands and arms). On the first landing we meet with the furious barking of the dog belonging to Randy (clerk and factotum at Meadville), who moved here in September. Randy's wife is a likeable and intelligent black woman. She has a little girl of a few years' age, and a second child is expected around Christmastime. Finally, the first sign of ''racial integration'' in our house . . . .

I find four boxes full of letters, periodicals, books, and—above all—advertisements. I spend several hours opening packets and tossing into the wastebasket those things I know wouldn't interest me, or which I won't have time to read.

9 October

At 10:00, meeting in my office with Conyers from the *Encyclopedia of Religion* in order to prepare the agenda for the work session this afternoon. Discussions, *en petit comité,* from 2:00 till 5:00. I am pleased that the whole group—Joe Kitagawa, Martin Marty, Conyers, and his secretary—accept my suggestions.

This evening Charles Adams arrives from Canada and Jacob Needleman from California.

10 October

This morning and afternoon, work sessions with the editorial board of the *Encyclopedia.* It's curious that I don't feel tired, although I have to find solutions to numerous problems (the allocation of the materials, the number of words allotted to the central subjects, the names of the most suitable contributors, etc.).

I have a great satisfaction: the *Encyclopedia* will be truly an international work. Savants from all continents will contribute, and from Europe we shall invite specialists not only from the West, but also from Russia, Romania, Hungary, Poland, etc.

11 October

This morning, from 10:00 till 11:00, the last conference of the editorial board. It takes place in room number 1 at the Quadrangle Club. I remember, all of a sudden, that exactly twenty-five years ago we lived here, in this very room. We had arrived on October 1 from New York. We believed that we would be staying in Chicago just seven or eight months!

The weather—incomparably beautiful, as it was then too. *As it was then* . . . .One thing gave me courage then: the thought that I'd soon return to Paris.

14 October

Lisette telephones to tell us that my name appears in *Le Petit Larousse,* 1981 edition. The honor surprises me, but I'm pleased too (especially for the joy it gives Christinel and others).

17 October

I held the first seminar yesterday. Depressed at how little the new students know *in general,* not just in the history of religions! If I'd found such ignorance in my students of 1956–1957, probably I wouldn't have stayed in Chicago.

20 October

In a study about the most recent scientific methods and discoveries, I find this anecdote which, the author asserts, "may serve as an example of complementary approaches." Felix Bloch and Werner Heisenberg, on a walk along the shore, discussed problems of physics. Bloch was reporting to Heisenberg some new ideas about certain mathematical structures of space when Heisenberg, his mind drifting into complementary avenues of experience, exclaimed: Space is blue and birds are flying in it!

10 November

Only today did I realize that my Monnier-Williams Sanskrit dictionary has disappeared. When? I consulted it the last time in May. Who could have taken it? Almost anyone can enter my office . . . .

This is the third copy I've lost since coming to Chicago.

16 November

I shall have to conclude *Histoire des croyances religieuses* with a general presentation of the religious experiences and crises of the entire globe; but I shall have to present also the *theoretical* (philosophical) understanding of religion *today*, after so many interpretations and so much *history*. After materialism and positivism, after Marx, Freud, and the other brilliant reductionists, after the "God-is-dead" theology—what can be said *today* about religious experience?

For the first time in history it is possible to do this.

20 November

Schiller wrote to Goethe on 2 November 1795: "Never has it been otherwise, and never will it be otherwise." This statement contradicts the whole *Zeitgeist* of the Enlightenment and the scientific and industrial revolutions, but it contradicts also the "natural" optimism of Goethe. The volumes of the Goethe-Schiller correspondence are lacking in the Meadville library. I shall have to search for them at Regenstein (but *when?*). Curious to find out what Goethe replied.

25 November

The book of Allan Ludwig, *Graven Images: New England Stone Carving and Its Symbols* (Wesleyan University Press, Middletown: 1966), is captivating. I have copied many inscriptions. Am surprised and fascinated at the freedom the first generations of colonists enjoyed in New England. See what a poor colonist was allowed to say in his funerary inscription:

> Here lie I at the chapel door;
> Here lie I because I'm poor.
> The further in, the more you pay;
> Here lie I as warm as they.

6 December

From 4:00 till 6:00, reception organized by John Shopp in Swift Commons, sponsored by Harper and Row, publishers, to "honor" me on the occasion of the appearance of volume 1 of my memoirs: *Autobiography, 1907–1937; Journey East, Journey West*. I sign fifty copies. I try to smile, I talk with several "admirers," but I do not succeed in participating in this editorial operation. (On the telephone for the past two weeks I tried in vain to convince Shopp that the reception made no sense.)

10 December

I learn of the death of Sergiu Al-George on November 10. Cardiac collapse—although the cardiogram made the day before was perfect. The news depresses me beyond words. Not only because I admired him as a scholar and valued him as a man and a friend, but also because, exasperated as I am by the rhythm in which I am drafting *Histoire* III, I had decided to ask him to help me in writing a part of the long chapter about medieval and postmedieval India. No one else could do it (that is, present the material with competence and with an interpretation very close to my own).

Romanian Indianistics has disappeared with the death of one man.

17 December

This evening, a mood of terrible sadness. In Poland, the "army" has intervened. Tens of thousands arrested, and all that we imagined—because, for several days, Poland has been completely isolated from the rest of the world (i.e., from the West). And nothing can be done. The alternative: the risk of an atomic war. Once again the Soviets have demonstrated that they do not intend to give up *anything* of what they have conquered or have yet to conquer.

PALM BEACH, *23 December*

We arrived last night, at 10:00. Warm: 70° F.! Lisette arrived twelve hours earlier. We are staying at the Ocean Echo. After a quarter of an hour of conversation, I go out for a stroll on the ocean shore. Suddenly, I feel ridiculous dressed as I am, with a sweater and overcoat. In the night, insomnia. The first in a good many years.

I write at random, anything that passes through my head. I want to re-accustom myself to the *Journal,* to writing. It's been many weeks since I worked "with great efficiency" (as I used to like to say). Something's happened to me, but I can't seem to put my finger on it precisely. Is it arthritic-rheumatic fatigue, or the result of the treatments with gold salts? Is it the detachment from *Histoire* III which compels me to write the last chapters of the *second half* of the book without enthusiasm? At any rate, never before have I known such fatigue, such detachment and indifference. If I were to record *exactly* and completely all I've suffered in the past twelve or fourteen months (the injections of gold, the parallel treatment with six pills per day, the physical therapy, etc.), perhaps the eventual reader would understand the state of abulia in which I find myself.

In addition (and even more painful): I can't write without the "apparatus" which protects my joints, I see less and less clearly, etc., etc.

I take advantage of this superb day (but it *is* too warm: 80°!) to write, noting the most recent events and "attacks." The seminar with Frank Reynolds was rather successful. (I told the students one evening how I began these "joint seminars" with Paul Tillich in 1965. And after his death, I continued them as we had begun them: Wednesday evenings, from 7:30 till 10:00, in the Curtis Room, here in Meadville). In contrast, I worked at *Histoire* III in a rather mediocre mood. I've finished transcribing the chapter on medieval Judaism, begun in Paris. Have started the chapter "Islam II," but it goes hard.

This morning, a long walk along the beach. The same lizards on the walls, the same orange butterflies hovering among the bushes—and the waves, too, the same. And yet, no trace of melancholy, although the years are passing, passing.

Lydia invited us to have lunch at the country club. As soon as we returned home, I went to bed and slept for almost an hour. A curious feeling of fatigue. I'm reminded of my youth: the first days at the seashore tired me as much as climbing a mountain.

Then, a long walk around the city. In the evening, Christinel and I dine at the Hearth of Palm Beach. Lisette wasn't feeling very well. She remains in her room and reads the pages of *Le Quotidien de Paris* devoted to my most recent books.

I'm beginning to return to normal. At Chicago, I was simply ill—and wouldn't admit it. I have to get well. I want to attempt all that lies within my powers.

Will note a few details: for the last ten or twelve days, incapable of working. Have reread (for the third time) Bielchowsky's biography of Goethe and *Dichtung und Warheit*. Surprised this time by the exasperating egocentrism of my dear Goethe.

24 December

Superb day! It's almost too warm: 84°! I try to remember: it was a day like this, warm, beautiful, in summer (July? August?) in a café, surely somewhere in Ticino. At a neighboring table, a man still rather young, with a short salt-and-pepper beard, was explaining to his companion that some large number of varieties of coleoptera had disappeared from Europe "in about forty years." I was troubled by the certainty with which he specified, slowly and with emphasis, "in about forty years."

25 December

Superb! Warm. Long walk on Gulfstream Road. I walked looking down at the sidewalk to avoid stepping on the lizards watching for little flies in the full sunlight. Thus I spied, half covered by a banyan leaf, a gold pendant. Shaking off the dirt, I saw it had thirteen little sapphires in it. The first "precious object" I've ever found in my long life.

(Note: But it didn't bring me luck. A few weeks later Christinel was found to have a malignant tumor, and before her operation, she gave the gold pendant to a church in our neighborhood to sell and use for the relief of the poor.)

29 December

Today was the warmest day yet: 85°F. Our room, with its four windows, all toward the sun, was as hot as the railway station in Avignon in the middle of August. Unbearable. We went down to the garden and stretched out on chaise longues in the shade. Not a cloud in the sky since we came.

31 December

In the past few days I've resumed work. I write with great effort, and almost illegibly. But I shall try later to dictate these pages to Christinel.

PALM BEACH, *1 January 1982*

This evening, at Lydia's, but we return at 9:30. As every day, walks on the ocean beach and Middle Road. The weather has been, day after day, unbelievable: 80°, with a sea breeze.

I've been thinking constantly of a novella, but the "subject" keeps changing, so I haven't dared to start writing.

Today, in order to mark the beginning of the year, I redacted the pages about Sohrawardî. I write with the same difficulty. I have to rest my hand every five minutes or so.

CHICAGO, *11 January*

Yesterday was the coldest day in the history of Chicago. The headlines on the front page of the *Chicago Tribune:* "THE COLDEST DAY IN HISTORY: −28°" (with the "windchill" at −80°). The streets are empty. In a quarter of an hour I saw only one pedestrian pass on Woodlawn Avenue.

20 February

Last night I discover that Christinel has a temperature of 39.9°C. I call the doctor. At 11:30 we go to Billings. The two doctors come. She has to stay here; they don't understand the cause of the fever.

21 February

I learn of the death of Gershom Scholem. Christinel is still at the hospital. They haven't given her the reason for the fever of yesterday and the day before.

1 March

For the past three days, Christinel has been much better. No fever, good appetite. Probably she'll come home tomorrow. But Dr. Herbst says that she must resume X-ray therapy.

21 March

Last night (Saturday) at 11:00 Christinel could no longer stand the pain caused by an infected tooth. I telephoned doctors (two of them!), and they suggested we go immediately to Emergency Services at Billings. Fortunately, Sanda Loga was with us, and she took us in her car (as she did also on the night I discovered Christinel had a fever).

Some are sleeping with their heads on others' laps or leaning back in their chairs. Other persons are smoking aggressively. Still others are pacing anxiously in the hall.

At 12:30 the dentist, summoned by Dr. X., approached us. The extraction of the tooth was, according to Christinel, very skillfully effected. He gave her a number of pills to take during the night.

22 March

Unfortunately, the excess of medicines has provoked a serious stomach upset. Christinel can't eat or drink anything.

27 March

Last night the radiator stopped heating. This morning Christinel has a cold. It's going to be a terrible weekend for me! All our troubles lately have happened on weekends.

18 April

I'm in no condition to think about anything except Christinel's operation. At 4:00 I go to Billings to tell her how the "reception" went. (I sense that she is beginning to be anxious about the operation.)

19 April

Christinel was operated on today, at noon. (It was supposed to have been at 8:30, but two "emergencies" intervened.) At 2:30 Dr. Herbst telephones that the operation had the best possible results. Christinel will remain for an hour or two in the recovery room, then will be taken to her own room, where Charlotte Collier is waiting for her.

I went to see her at 6:00 (Dr. Herbst advised me not to go any earlier). She had fallen asleep after the last shot for pain and healing the incision. But when I was squeezing her hand, she recognized me in her sleep and said something (in Romanian?) which I failed to understand.

I have engaged a private nurse to spend the nights with her.

20 April

Last night at 10:30 the nurse called me on the phone. Christinel wanted to speak to me. She asked if I had eaten dinner, and where. (Her great fear—that alone, I won't be able to take care of myself.)

Also last night I found out from Claire Lacocque that Ileana Cuşa telephoned twice.

Today at 11:00, at the hospital. Charlotte was already there. Christinel looks better, although she hasn't drunk a drop of liquid in thirty-six hours. She knew about the telephone calls from Paris. Also, Dr. Bloncourt has spoken by phone with Dr. Herbst. Now, at 2:45, telephone call from Paris. Paul Barbăneagră wants to know, *in detail,* how the operation went.

Christinel's room is full of flowers—and at my office the telephone rings continually. People are so good . . . . This love has given Christinel much courage.

21 April

In the morning I telephone Giza to give her the good news. Then I go to the hospital. Christinel is improving little by little. Today she was allowed a *thimbleful* of water.

22 April

The weather remains beautiful, but cold. I begin a novella (probable title: *Exile*). Between 3:00 and 6:00 I write over twenty pages. But there is much padding.

24 June

Christinel is becoming herself again, little by little. Although the pains continue, she takes the narcotic tablets only very rarely.

PARIS,· *June*

I should convince myself that, being past seventy-five, all the infirmities I suffer—arthritis, fatigue of the eyes (from the cataract?), drowsiness, atony, lack of interest in works begun—all these can't be *cured* (or at least some of them can't). There's no use hoping, forming illusions. It's probable that my "infirmities" are just the concrete expression of old age.

There's only one thing I regret: that I didn't plan in time and make the effort to finish *Histoire* in the years 1975–1980.

EGYALIÈRES, *5 July*

Friday, 2 July, Sorin took us to Gare de Lyon. We left at 10:55 and arrived at Avignon at 3:40—almost two hours early. But not by that magnificent train, the Mistral (which has been discontinued). At the station, Ileana and Gabrielle. Superb weather. At Mas du Tilleul we find Maria and Cornelia (Ileana's mother and sister).

The next day, Saturday, 3 July, Thérèse Delpech and François Furet arrive (I had just read the latter's book, *L'Atelier de l'histoire*). Furet and Cornelia are leaving on the fourth of September.

The weather remains superb. Third session at the pool (because I musn't swim too long at one time). I don't have much desire to work, but I withdraw into the tower and begin the redacting of the chapter "London, 1940," for the second volume of the *Autobiography*. I write four pages.

10 July

I have worked almost every day; have written between four and six pages daily. But I corrected the chapter already written (1938) and have set aside a number of "political" details which would not interest anyone but Romanians (the pages eliminated can be published in a possible Romanian edition).

More seriously, although I write with an elastic bandage on it, my right hand tires after only thirty minutes.

14 July

In the past several days I've continued to work: I eliminate, rework, correct, summarize. Last night, with Dr. Bloncourt and Marie-Claude, at Orange. An hour by car. We dine at a restaurant built in the form of a cave; then, at the Roman amphitheater, *La Forza del*

Destino, with Caballé. Three hours on stone (we brought cushions) without being able to lean against anything. Very stiff. The performance lasted until almost 1:00. We return at 2:00. And immediately—sharp pains all down my spine. With difficulty I get out of the car. I can hardly climb the stairs to our room. I don't know how many pills I swallow.

Today, the pains have diminished, but they increase as soon as I remain on a chair for more than twenty or thirty minutes.

In the tower, I succeed nevertheless in wrapping up the chapter on London.

19 July

Last evening Marie-France and Monica arrived. Still no news from Virgil Tănase. But Monica seems optimistic, and it could be that Virgil's alive, under the protection of the French secret service.

26 July

Since our arrival at Eygalières, I have walked between two and three kilometers daily with Christinel. Sometimes in two walks. I look at my watch; we return after thirty, sixty, or seventy-five minutes (but we stop along the way). Christinel *has* to walk and, especially, to climb and descend stairs, but she musn't tire herself. Today we went to the village (two and a half kilometers). We rested at a café.

1 August

Yesterday I resumed work on the novella begun last spring at Chicago; I wrote and transcribed three pages. Today I wrote six pages, and it's finished. The title (provisional?): *La umbra unui crin* [In the shade of a lily]. But I don't know if I can count it as one of my successful novellas.

2 August

Yesterday Christinel read *La umbra unui crin*, and she didn't like it. I reread the whole text today and added another six pages. I think I've finished it this time.

August

Depressed by how little and how badly I work. I haven't succeeded even in reading the few books on Byzantine mysticism I brought with me. Not even in summarizing, in French, certain paragraphs from my study on popular religion ["History of Religions and 'Popular' Cultures," *History of Religions* 20, no. 1, (Spring 1980)], for a chapter in *Histoire* III. Moreover, the same old syndrome: detachment from *Histoire* and the *Encyclopedia of Religion*, procrastination with respect to the *Autobiography* (it is true, I don't have with me, or at Paris, the *Journal* for the years 1941—1945, Portugal-Paris). What's even worse is the difficulty with which I succeed in writing a few almost indecipherable lines.

I've given up the pleasure of bathing in the pool because it seemed to me the joints of my hands were becoming stiffer.

PARIS, *1–2 September*

Sensational news: V. Tănase is alive! I read all the papers. Fantastic—and yet, an excellent adventure novel.

On 31 August in the evening we dined with Marie-France and Mihnea Berendei; on 1 September with the Ieruncas, Paul Goma, and Marie-France. We discuss—or, more precisely, we listen to discussions about Virgil Tănase and "Monsieur Z," the one who was supposed to execute Goma and Tănase.

10 September

I breathe a sigh of relief today, giving some hundred books to Andrei Bordeianu and an equal number to the church on rue Jean de Beauvais (to be sold or kept?). My hope: to "liquidate" another two to three hundred volumes before leaving. And if I have enough courage and strength, I'll do the same thing, but on a larger scale, at Chicago. I should keep only four to five hundred volumes and my own works in various editions and translations.

11 September

Ruggiero Ruggieri writes me from Rome: I have been accorded the Premio Mediteraneo (two million lire) on the condition that I be

present at Palermo on 20 and 21 October, because the prize is awarded
only in person. I shall telephone tomorrow that "unfortunately" I
cannot accept. On 2 October we leave for New York, on the seventh
we'll be in Chicago, and on the twentieth (!) I must give the lecture long
ago promised to Davíd Carrasco. An American scholar would not be
impressed by a triple crossing of the Atlantic in three weeks, but in the
state of fatigue in which I find myself, for me it would be impossible.

But refusing any "honors" in foreign countries and any dialogue or
interview on radio or television (as I had to refuse the week-long
entretien proposed by Chostel) limits my "publicity" to a minimum. I
realize that my publishers aren't too happy about it.

SUMMER—

I promised Siegfried Unseld long ago—last spring—an introduction to the ten volumes of my *Werke*. I must, by all means, write it
before we return to Chicago. What an excellent opportunity for me to
disclose and comment on the profound unity of my writings, both the
literary and historico-philosophical! I've spoken in passing about this
complementarity (the last time in *L'Épreuve du labyrinthe*), but I've
never treated the subject in depth.

Unfortunately, I won't be able to do it now: the abulia continues, and
the effort required for me to write tires me out. (I should accustom
myself to the dictaphone.) I shall, therefore, reproduce excerpts from
the *Autobiography*, from a lecture published in *Criterion*, and from
L'Épreuve.

I note also these details: (1) the volume of the *Werke* scheduled for
autumn has been posponed (*sine die?*) because of the introduction; (2)
the two volumes of Duerr's *Festschrift* have been postponed until
winter, for reasons I don't exactly understand. I'm afraid that both
Unseld and Duerr are hesitating—lest they reopen the old matter of my
"fascism."

BOULDER, COLORADO, *24–26 October*

We've been here three days, but not until today did we take an
automobile ride up into the Rocky Mountains. Too bad that an hour after
we set out, it began to rain. Last spring I accepted the invitation of my

former student Davíd Carrasco: a public lecture (I read the long text "Waiting for the Dawn") and three seminars. Surprise: an immense hall, and it was full; the folding wall had to be opened. Over twelve hundred persons, the majority students. Peggy and Burton Feldmann came also. Then we all had dinner at the restaurant of the Holiday Inn, where we are staying.

I note a few other details: dinner at the home of another student (Fred _____); lecture on the twenty-sixth; cocktail party on the twenty-seventh. We return 29 October.

November

I feel worse and worse; drowsy, no desire to work, tired. I'm sure that the treatment with gold isn't agreeing with me. I have no more pains, but my right hand remains as stiff as before. I write with enormous difficulty. In addition, the cataract has progressed. I hardly manage to read: I can do better without the glasses, holding my face almost against the page.

And in spite of everything, I persist in believing in the "initiatory" meaning of these sufferings and debilities. I'm not just thinking of death. At my age, that's no longer a problem. The "initiation" pertains to *something else:* a "new life," i.e., a total regeneration which reveals to me another kind of creativity. I must get out of this pen of petty preoccupations in which I've been enclosed, without realizing it, for so many years.

15 November

Professor Robert Ellwood, a former pupil of mine from fifteen or sixteen years ago, writing to thank me for *Ordeal by Labyrinth*, tells me that he was in Calcutta recently, "and made it a point to walk along Ripon Street, where you had lived . . . . Needless to say, it's no more a European area or what it was, but colorful and interesting. I also spent some time at the Theosophical Society at Adyar, Madras."

Winter

I read long ago (perhaps in J. H. Fabre) about the courtship of scorpions. As long as they are "engaged," the scorpion male and his chosen one walk *en se tenant par la prince*—and these walks sometimes have a surprising duration and morphology. A few days ago, meeting with L. V., a specialist in zoology, I asked him for details. Smiling ironically, L. V. stated that this "courtship of scorpions," although real, is less interesting than we dilettantes imagine it. It is an anthropomorphizing of the sexual instinct. He told me that the "engagement" is only a phase preliminary to sexual union, etc. The "walking dance" is, of course, real—but *we* accord it the function and value of dance, etc., etc.

I was disappointed. But later I had to admit that he was, in a way, right. I thought: in just this way the historians of chemistry evaluate certain experiments of alchemists, for the simple reason that they see in them the prefiguration of later science, i.e., an embryonic chemistry. Actually, alchemists pursued different objectives from those of the chemists of the eighteenth of nineteenth centuries.

The depressing banality of the constant self-critical stance of the American intelligentsia. It is exasperating for a European to hear them (in academic surroundings) talking *exclusively* about the crimes and injustices of Americans.

"L'imagination n'a jamais trompé que les faibles ou les lâches, incapables de porter le poids d'un grand rêve." [The imagination has deceived only the weak or the cowardly, who are incapable of bearing the weight of a great dream.] (Bernanos, lignes écrites peu après la publication de *Sous le Soleil de Satan*.)

CHICAGO, *February 1983*

I still have to give away (to the library, friends, students) some three thousand books. So far I've given to the Meadville library over five hundred volumes and to students nearly one hundred. I shall have to give them all away within the year. Only then will I have space on my shelves for *my* books, manuscripts, and correspondence, the theses and studies about me, etc.

How simple it would be if I could donate *everything* to the Library of the Romanian Academy!

9 March

It's snowing. I have only to complete *État des questions* for chapter 38, and the book is finished. This chapter, the penultimate, is nothing to brag about. I wrote it with an immense effort, without any interest, tired and distracted before finishing the first page.

Yesterday evening, when I had transcribed the last page, I recalled the pericardiac attack of 9 March 1971, at Albion. I said to myself that the same thing could happen again tonight. Therefore, I am making an extra effort to finish the book.

I reread the *Journal* from January 1972 to the fall of 1973. I recall a great many initiatory details.

17 March

Yesterday evening the last session of the seminar with Paul Ricoeur was held. The title: "The Mythic." General discussion. At the end, the members of the seminar applauded. The fact is, this was my *last* class at the University of Chicago.

Finally, emeritus! (Yet not quite, because in 1983–1984 I shall be listed in the catalogue as "professor, on leave of absence.")

No trace of melancholy. I don't even try to recall the fall of 1956 when I came as visiting professor and to deliver the Haskell Lectures. Perhaps later I shall try to make an accounting of those twenty-seven years as a professor.

Anyhow, I don't regret that I remained at Chicago. Of this, too, Christinel was convinced long ago. Nowhere in Europe would I have had the freedom to teach what I wanted and as I wanted. And I wonder if my ideas would have become popular, as they have become long since in the U.S.A., only through my books written in Paris and later, possibly, translated into English.

20 March

How I dread to receive and open *now* packages of books, especially those I receive (very seldom) from Romania! I dread it first because I must decide if the book is worth giving to the Meadville library, or if I should store it in the attic (especially books written in Romanian) in anticipation of a "liquidation" (for Regenstein? Romanian friends and acquaintances?).

27 March

In *Cartea Vîlvelor*, a collection of folklore from the Apuseni Mountains, published by Maria Ionica (1982), a legend about "The Shepherd of the Wolves," collected on 4 December, 1979 begins this way: "Once upon a time there were hunters . . ." (193). The informant, age sixty-eight, spoke about the immediate past as if he were evoking a fabulous era. (Compare: "Once upon a time there were ogres . . ." [204].)

March

"Et cela, mon petit, pense que seul, en tant que Russe, j'étais alors en Europe *l'unique Européen*.. Je ne parle pas de moi, je parle de toute la pensée russe . . . ." (*L'Adolescent*, Editions Pléiade, 507). [And so, my little one, as a Russian I was the *only European* in Europe then. I am not speaking about myself; I am speaking about all Russian thought.] This vision of Dostoevski (developed in his Pushkin speech in 1880) ought to be adopted (but perhaps it has been already) by all Romanian writers in exile.

6 April

At 12:45, the lecture (forty-five minutes) which I promised long ago, in Swift Commons; as usual, immediately after dessert and coffee at the faculty-student Wednesday luncheon. The last time I addressed them, some four or five years ago, I spoke about *Histoire des idées religieuses*; this time, "My Career as Historian of Religions and Writer." I repeated what I've said on other occasions, improvising and reading random selections. The students seemed enthusiastic, as did also my professor-colleagues who were present.

The whole time I was obsessed by a single thought: that I was speaking for the last time in that room and that therefore I should make the effort to say something new and interesting. I don't believe I succeeded. On the contrary, this sense of obligation, of *having to*, made it difficult for me to concentrate.

8 April

I admit: I read with interest the studies of literary critics who use my studies in the history of religions in an intelligent and convincing way.

A few months ago there fell into my hands Edward J. Cronin's article, "Eliade, Joyce, and the Nightmare of History" (*Journal of the American Academy of Religion*, September 1982, 435–48). Excellent.

Yesterday I received from Bob M. Fusa (New Orleans) a long and fascinating article: "A Detective Story. The Influence of Mircea Eliade on Alejo Carpentier's *Los pasos perdidos*" (I don't know when it will be published). In this case the author demonstrates precisely the influence of my article "Symbolisme indien de l'abolition du temps" on the genesis and construction of the novel of the great Afro-Cuban writer. And he concludes the letter: "Thank you for your work in the history of religions, which has been invaluable to my research."

9 April

The bookstore on Fifty-seventh Street, The Green Door, has been closed. The owner would not extend the lease. Old Mrs. Staver had to sell the books at reduced prices. If only she had been able to sell them all!

Melancholy. Yet another "witness" to our lives in Chicago is gone. I met her first some twenty years ago (her husband, I believe, had recently died). I never passed the store windows without stopping and looking them over. The few books I bought locally, I bought from Staver's. I often wondered how she held out. Seldom did I see any customers in the store. And the store remained open until 10:00 at night.

9 May

Last night, after dinner with many professors (colleagues and former students of mine), I inaugurated the "mini-conference" on methodology in the history of religions with a lecture entitled "*Homo Faber* and *Homo Religiosus*: An Experiment in Method." The room: fuller than I've ever seen it. Jonathan Smith read an admirable and amusing "introduction" of fifteen minutes. I read my lecture rather well (Christinel assures me); enthusiastic applause.

I am glad that it happened this way. It was the *last public lecture* I shall give. My "swan song," as I told Christinel. I'll participate in discussions and seminars, but never will I present anywhere another public lecture.

10 May

Yesterday and today I listened—from 9:00 A.M. till 5:00 P.M.—to all the lectures, papers, and discussions. Yesterday, Michel Meslin and Ugo Bianchi spoke. Each lecture was followed by the observations of "respondents" and by discussion. Last night, Paul Ricoeur's lecture—dedicated, he said with some emotion, to "Mircea Eliade: master, colleague, and friend." Today, the lecture after dinner by Chuck Long.

There were at least twenty or twenty-two of my former students present. Some of them I hadn't seen in ten years. Last evening we invited a whole group to our apartment. Among those who came were Wendy, Larry Sullivan, and Kees Bolle (who reminded me of the years when he was a student and I would invite him in the evening for a glass of whiskey and we would talk for hours). Also Mac Ricketts (with whom I shall "work"tomorrow) and Sorin (fascinated by the "atmosphere" of the university, by the fact that I am so well-liked).

There is much else that could be added, but I'm tired. For three days I've been waking up at 7:00 and going to bed at 1:30 . . . .

13 May

I realize that the "mini-conference" on methodology was planned originally as a celebration of my retirement (becoming emeritus). But two months ago I requested the dean, Chris Gamwell, *not* to have a celebration for me. I assured him that I would be keeping the apartment for two more years, that I would continue to work in my office at Meadville (on *Autobiography* II, etc.), that I would hold work sessions on the *Encyclopedia here*, in Chicago.

I'm glad I persuaded him. Nothing was *said*. But the presence of so many former students of mine, the words spoken by Paul Ricoeur, the enthusiastic and emotional applause—all these showed that, actually, it *was* an observance in my honor. And a "good-bye" without tears.

20 May

Matei Calinescu comes with two young Romanian women who tell me that it's become impossible to live now in Romania, even ethnically.

May

"De ceux qui ne signent pas les manifestes on dit qu'ils ne s'intéressent pas à leur époque, ce qui de nos jours est tenu pour un délit; il arrive qu'on les insulte" (Montherlant, *Tous feux éteints*, 71). [Of those who do not sign manifestos it is said that they are not interested in their time, which in our day is taken for a crime; and they are sometimes even insulted.]

PARIS, 28 *June*

For several days, no desire to work. I read Siménon: almost two novels per day.

BRUSSELS, *12 July*

Dinu and Giza take us to the station. Very warm. Brussels. Evening at the Royal Windsor Hotel. Two rooms. We eat dinner in the Galerie at Taverna.

15 July

Very warm. We stroll in the Plaza. Lunch in Galerie de la Reine. Deluxe bookstore.

16 July

At 1:00 André and Claire Lacocque come to take us by car to Bruges. Snack in an outdoor restaurant. Then, by taxi for half an hour, to visit Ghent. Then, to Ostend. Stroll on the beach. We dine at The Club; very elegant.

Back in Brussels by 11:00 P.M.

PARIS, *July*

If it happens sometimes—less and less often—that I take the pen in hand to write something (a note, a memory), I am reminded of the pain I'll feel in my joints after the first words are written, and I ask myself if it's *worth* writing. Most of the time I decide it isn't.

CHICAGO, *8 November*

Am writing with immense difficulty. I finish reading *Bollingen: An Adventure in Collecting the Past*, William McGuire's monograph [Princeton, 1982]. Fascinating; and yet, for Christinel and me, melancholic. Too many memories.

14 November

To Dr. Sorensen again. I show him my hands and tell him that I can hardly write anymore. He has no other solution than ten more shots, weekly, of gold.

I must reconcile myself with this thought: I shall have to learn to dictate and to type with a few fingers of my left hand.

15 November

It is decided: Christinel will have a hernia operation on 28 November. A week in the hospital. We both hope this will get rid of the pains which torture her so much, especially after eating. There will be two operations, several months apart—because the hernia has appeared on the other side of the abdomen also.

19 November

Telephone call from Adriana Berger (she has been in Los Angeles since this summer). We invite her, at our expense, to come and stay here from January till 1 April 1984. She will help to put my library in order. Impossible for me to get things straightened out otherwise. I can't lift heavy books from the shelves, I can't rummage among the file folders. Packages of books and envelopes I open wherever I can. At Swift Hall, Mrs. Rehova Arthur picks up the scissors as soon as she sees me coming in the door.

Why have I been punished for—and through—those things I have loved all my life: books and writing?

20 November

Have finished putting the final touches to the text of my May lecture, "*Homo Faber* and *Homo Religiosus*."

Since returning to Chicago, I've done nothing but "trifles": correcting theses, articles for the *Encyclopedia*, etc.

24 November, Thanksgiving

Cold, windy. We are reminded of our first Thanksgiving, in 1956, at Harriet Platt's. We went by car, with the Charles Longs and the Kitagawas. Marvelous house on a wooded estate, some twenty miles from Chicago.

How beautiful this country was until a hundred years ago.

25 November

Tristan has received the Goncourt Prize; Christinel found out from Ileana, who telephoned from Paris. I'm as delighted as can be. I read *Les Égarés* with interest, in places with enthusiasm.

26 November

I leaf through the collections of *Îndreptar* and *Cuvântul în exil* in order to select several articles for the volume being prepared by C. Poghirc and possibly also for Gallimard (to be translated by A. Paruit).

Melancholy. Aggravated by the difficulty I have in penning these lines.

27 November

A horrible day. Cold, rainy, windy. Christinel enters the hospital for her hernia operation, which will take place tomorrow morning.

28 November

The cold rain continues, gradually turning to snow.

Christinel had surgery at 10:00. When I see her at 3:00 she looks very well. Fortunately, she has a spacious room with a large window overlooking the garden. When she is alone, she reads *Les Égarés*.

11 January 1984

Adriana Berger arrived last night from New York. We have found her a room in the apartment of Richard Stern's former wife.

Today at 2:00, with dean Chris Gamwell, at Regenstein. Meeting with Rosenthal, director of Special Collections (to which I donated a number of books and offprints some twelve or thirteen years ago). Then Rosenthal comes to Meadville and our apartment at 5711 Woodlawn to inspect the collections of letters and manuscripts.

The plan: in a few days he will send several young men to pick up all these materials and deposit them in Regenstein. The second step: they will take away thousands of offprints (from my works and those of others) and the first lot of books. The third step: the manuscript of the *Autobiography*. Later, the notebooks of the *Journal*—to photocopy them.

20 January

Last week they carted away the correspondence from home and from Meadville, plus the small boxes of offprints. My office is unrecognizable now. But I quickly realize that in her desire to "clean up" my room, Adriana has rearranged the books on my shelves, crowding them together, changing their locations—so that I can't find anything I want to consult or read!

A new kind of despair.

28 January

Too sad, too depressed, and too tired to record in this notebook the episodes and adventures in the saga of the "dispersion" of my library. Adriana has quarreled with Müller, Rosenthal's assistant, so she is working now in one of the classrooms here at Meadville. Sometimes she remains until late at night.

At the same time, she has to gather together the files with my articles and those of my critics, and "classify" them.

8 February

I have written to the Romanian ambassador in Washington, Malița, proposing to donate a part of my library to the Library of the

Romanian Academy. The idea was suggested to me last fall by Poghirc, who assured me that even if many publications (*History of Religions*, etc.) will be forbidden to the public, he believes they won't be destroyed.

I have kept a copy of my letter.

12 February

It's hard for me to understand (or even imagine) how furiously I'm disposing of my library. Almost every week I give away dozens of books (sometimes fifty or sixty), a part to the library at Meadville, a part to the Library of the Romanian Academy (I hope!), the rest to Regenstein or to colleagues and former students of mine.

And yet, the shelves of my office look the same: still laden with books. It is true, the steel filing cabinets filled with periodicals and offprints have disappeared, along with the heaps of books that covered them.

21 February

Since I began "selecting" materials, I can't do anything productive. I barely manage to write a few letters—short, insipid, and probably illegible.

Fortunately, I've read and checked a large number of articles for the *Encyclopedia*.

1 March

This morning Christinel underwent surgery again. Dr. Herbst telephoned to tell me everything is perfect. I went to see her at 5:00 this afternoon. She didn't seem like someone who had been operated on only a few hours before.

This evening, at the Kitagawas, for a "family dinner." Christinel, in very good spirits, telephoned them.

I write with increasing difficulty. I *must* find a solution! Perhaps the cortisone shots in the joints, which Dr. Sorensen told me about . . . .

2 March

As was expected, today, the "day after" the operation—Christinel feels worse. She has a little fever. Probably an infection.

Antibiotics, directly into the vein. After ten hours, her temperature falls to 37.°C.

3 March

Christinel is better. Her temperature is falling. I can't work. (The same old story: I'm living among the letters and notes of twenty and twenty-five years ago.)

5–8 March

Mac Ricketts has come for three days (he is our guest at the Quadrangle Club), in order to complete his biographical data. He has obtained a grant from the National Endowment for the Humanities which will allow him a year without courses and several trips (he will come to Paris in October). All these things for the book he is preparing to write: *Mircea Eliade: His Life and Works* [*Mircea Eliade: The Romanian Roots 1907–1945* (Boulder: East European Monographs, 1988).] He tells me about things that happened and conversations he had in Romania (where he spent three months in 1981).

Accompanied by Adriana, he examines the materials gathered but not yet classified in Special Collections. Then he comes to Meadville and rummages through the stacks of books destined for Regenstein Library. He selects a dozen or so boóks he did not succeed in finding in Romania.

But the true "research," alone or assisted by Adriana, he carried out for six or eight hours per day, in a classroom in Meadville, in all the packets of articles, reviews, studies, etc. accumulated in my office, going through them attentively, "one by one." All that he lacks, he photocopies (although, as he acknowledges, he possesses the most extensive "Eliadeana collection" in the world—because he transcribed or photocopied at the Library of the Romanian Academy over one thousand articles and book reviews published between 1921 and 1940).

Two evenings we dined together. He keeps asking me questions. There are periods still only partially understood; for example, the accusations or allusions to my "Nazism" (anti Semitism) in the years 1938 and 1939. I try to explain; I recall for him certain articles, conversations, and events of those years.

All these things leave me exhausted. For almost two months I've been living "in the past." I can't resume the writing of the *Autobiography*, interrupted on 5 January, on the eve of our departure from Palm Beach.

At all costs, tomorrow, 9 March, I will shut myself away at home for a few hours, and I will write!

8 March

In the afternoon, Christinel returns from the hospital. She brought with her some of the flowers that brightened her room.

At 2:30, Mac Ricketts leaves.

17 March

The whole day lost checking over the files of correspondence arranged by Adriana. Then, in the evening, I prepare the second "donation" of books (the majority of them history, philology, and art history) for Mrs. Perciali. They will come to the apartment tomorrow and load them into their car. Then they will go to Meadville, where I have several boxes reserved for them. And yet, in spite of all this, the two libraries remain full; heaps of books on the floor.

But I have also the sentiment that I am anticipating the "breaking up" which will take place after our deaths.

20 March

I've begun to carry out the collections of journals destined for the Library of the Romanian Academy: *East and West*, *Journal Asiatique*, *Temenos*, *Journal of Indo-European Studies*, *Indo-Iranian Journal*, etc. I have stored them on the top floor, in a dark corner. I hope they don't tempt any of the rare visitors to that remote and dusty attic.

22 March

I receive, finally, an answer to my letter to Mircea Maliţa. He apologizes for the delay (moreover, the letter took ten days to travel from Washington to Chicago), but he has been busy, etc. Obviously he had to wait for instructions from Bucharest, that is, from Ceauşescu. He is agreeable, and he asks if I can see him between 1 and 3 May, when he will be in Chicago.

The only thing that interests me is to see the stacks of journals and books which I have laid aside for the Romanian Academy loaded up and carried away.

31 March

There's no doubt now that the breaking up of my library and, especially, the rearrangement of the manuscripts and the classification of the correspondence was a very big mistake. Perhaps the most serious error of the last twenty-five years! Not only have I not been able to do anything, but this daily schedule (rechecking, answering Adriana's queries, etc.) has exhausted me.

4 April

Last night, pains in my left ankle. (Curiously—twelve to fifteen hours since the last injection of gold.) I can scarcely drag myself to the bathroom, to take two Tylenol tablets. In the morning the pain persists, but by leaning on the umbrella, I succeed in reaching my office in Meadville. As usual, Adriana is at work. Dozens of files on the floor of the room next door; in the office there awaits me on the desk a large packet of letters, almost all from 1983. I begin to classify them, but I can't stand it for more than a half hour. I return home then, limping.

I can't do anything. Can't even read. A few weeks ago the pains passed within twenty-four hours. I hope they will this time too . . . .

5 April

All day, in bed, sleepy (I had to take Tylenol with codeine). Dr. Sorensen advised me the last time: rest, rest! Anyway, I walk with much difficulty, leaning on the umbrella.

I can't do anything. In order not to exasperate Christinel (who is still struggling, herself, five weeks after her operation, with pains of all sorts), I pretend to be concentrating on a collection of stamps which I haven't opened in several years.

6 April

Finally, the pains have gone. But I'm being careful. I walk to Swift Hall leaning on the cane which Etienette brought me this morning.

When I return, I go first to Meadville. Adriana had assured Christinel by phone that I wouldn't recognize my office! Indeed, I *don't* recognize it! She has opened two steel filing cabinets, placed all the offprints and books they contained on the floor, "arranged" all the books that were on chairs on shelves, etc., etc. To keep from exploding, I return home. In vain have I tried to sleep, throwing myself on the couch. I've been laid low by a series of misfortunes. For the nth time she ransacks and "reorganizes" my library, files, and notes. It will take at least a week for me to reorient myself to the new "organization" of my library. But weak as I am, I can't even pick up a heavy book. I'll have to ask several students to assist me.

10 April

Mike Maliszenski ("Aliosa") shows me a newspaper clipping: G. Tucci died on Thursday, 5 April.

Terrible sadness. Our last meeting: September 1981; we embraced when we parted. Memories: the first meeting in Dasgupta's house in Bhowanipore, in the winter of 1929, and all that followed.

How I regret having lost the *Journal* from those years! (Perhaps it will be discovered later, but what good will that do?) Tucci was eighty-nine.

13 April

I receive, forwarded from New York (Macmillan, *Encyclopedia of Religion*), a letter of 23 March from Gherardo Gnoli. He informs me: "Confidentially, since Professor Tucci's condition in the past months has, unfortunately, worsened, we can no longer hope for any improvement."

Sadly, I think about those "last months." Had he sunk into senility? Or, as I hope, was it only a matter of a physical degeneration?

This evening, with some twenty-five colleagues, "Dutch treat" dinner at the Thai restaurant. Frank and Mani Reynolds organized this dinner—an occasion for us to talk with one another. But at a table ten yards long, you can't talk to anyone but those sitting near you. A rush of emotion when, at the end, we sing in Frank's honor, "For he's a jolly good fellow!" Suddenly, I found myself in Calcutta, at 82 Ripon Street or in the restaurant in Chinatown. I was just twenty-two . . . . On the way home, I say to myself: I ought to be thinking about our departure. It's time to change, if not my "galaxy" (as I've gotten used to saying), then at least the city and the "milieu." Paris again, for example, or Provence, or Italy.

19 April

Rosenthal comes so we can discuss a "few problems" in connection with the "special collection." The last time he proposed photocopying the *Journal* and giving me the copy, keeping the original at Regenstein. But this means a box of at least forty-five pounds of paper. He understands immediately; the only important thing, he says, is that we protect the *Journal* against risks (especially since I'll be traveling, as I did last summer, with some five or six notebooks, in France and Italy). Therefore, he will come next week to take the fifty-six notebooks, and, he assures me, he will photocopy them in a few days (forty-one hundred pages). After that, I shall keep the originals at my office, and in the act of donation I will specify that, upon my death, they will be deposited at Regenstein. The photocopy will be sent someday, perhaps, to the Library of the Romanian Academy, or to some other institution in the homeland.

All these discussions and plans exhaust me. I feel tireder than ever, melancholy, depressed.

20 April

I have requested Handoca to subscribe to *România literară* for me. (It's the only review from the homeland that I receive—since the end of March—and read. I'm surprised, but mostly just amused, by the fact that my name has almost completely disappeared. No longer are there book reviews and articles, as in past years. And this has happened in the year when, in Germany, Peter Duerr has edited a *Festschrift* in three volumes, with some fifty or sixty contributors. (I may be mistaken about the number; I don't have the books in front of me and I can't make a count of them.)

25 April

I finish, finally, a small and uninspired obituary for Giuseppe Tucci, for *History of Religions* [24 no. 2 (November 1984): 157–59]. It took me three or four afternoons (true, I worked only two or three hours each day) to write, and, above all, to copy in a legible hand, the eight pages, almost three of which are bibliographic notes . . . .

Writing has become for me a torture. At every word written, my joints crack, and many times I have to stop a few moments and *rest*!

Bruce Lincoln came to see me at the office early in the afternoon. I showed him the first lot of books I've prepared for him: almost all Germanic literature which I've collected, beginning in Lisbon. (He came today, Sunday, 29 April, at lunchtime, and carried them away.) The second lot—some fifty or sixty volumes (Dumézil, Italian scholars, etc.)—I shall send him at the end of May. A rare satisfaction: to know that all these books which were so dear to me will remain from now on in the library of Bruce Lincoln—one of the most brillant and creative of my former students.

Friday, 27 April

Reception and dinner, given by the faculty, with the president, Hanna Gray, as a guest of honor. (For the first time, Christinel does not participate in such a ceremony; after the two-hour concert we attended downtown, she doesn't dare sit for more than an hour at a time on a chair. And also for the first time, we aren't inviting the group of friends and colleagues to our place for cognac, Scotch, and conversation on Saturday evening.)

In the evening, a tornado warning. While we are eating dinner, the thunderstorm breaks out suddenly. We don't dare to return to Swift Hall for the panel session: "ASSR in Retrospect and Prospect." Two older members, Joe Kitagawa and Kenneth Morgan, evoke the beginnings of the organization (the American Society for the Study of Religion). Three others, younger, discuss the future. A curious yet stimulating impression: I sensed that my "role and function" have begun to be, if not forgotten, at least pushed into the past: See the admirable title of the article by Ninian Smart of several years ago in *Numen* [25:2 (1978)]: "Beyond Eliade: The Future of Theory in Religion." Of course. It would be depressing if we kept doing the same thing over and over.

Saturday, 28 April

As usual, I attend the morning session. At 2:30 Seymour Cain comes to see me at the office, and we talk till 3:15. Then, to Swift Hall; Kurt Rudolf speaks about "Religious Studies and the Religious Situation in Eastern Europe." (Some wonder if he'll return to his chair at Leipzig.)

Sunday, April 29

I arrived at 10:15 (actually 11:15, because last night Daylight Savings Time began). I was able to hear a part of Panikkar's observations. Then, the hand-shaking, but only about half the membership was still there. Very probably I won't try to shake hands with anyone at the close of a future meeting.

April

I don't remember now whether or not I recorded in this notebook that Hans Peter Duerr has sent me the third and final volume of the *Festschrift* on which he has been working for several years: *Die Mitte der Welt: Aufsätze zu Mircea Eliade* (Suhrkamp Verlag). The second volume, *Sehnsucht nach dem Ursprung zu Mircea Eliade* (Syndikat, 1983, almost six hundred pages), impressed some of my "admirers" for the critical, "negative" articles it contained. The first volume, of more modest proportions, appeared last summer: *Alcheringa oder die beginnende Zeit*, at Qumran Verlag, a publishing house I'd never heard of.

I wanted very much to record these bibliographic details because, aside from a few bookstores and journalists in Germany, no one knows about this three-volume *Festschrift*. Perhaps some here in the United States do know, because Edward Shils and other Americans are included among the contributors. Information about the books can't be published in Romania, while Radio Free Europe becomes harder and harder to hear there.

5 May

I'm horrified realizing what's happened to me in the past several months: I scarcely succeed in writing a page or two per day. But all I write has to be corrected and rewritten, however "modest" the content may be. True, I'm continually harassed (meetings, reports in connection with articles for the *Encyclopedia*, etc.). Not to speak of my health: the pain in my joints has gotten worse, I feel tired all the time, I'm beginning to forget from one day to the next . . . . I believe the only thing I could write with pleasure—and rather rapidly, too—is the *Autobiography*.

15 May

Yesterday evening at 7:00 a commercial representative from the embassy, Gh. Folescu, came to take the first cartons (three cardboard boxes full of offprints—these in addition to the hundreds of offprints I sent to Regenstein). He will return tomorrow, at the same hour, with an assistant in order to carry away several thousand copies of journals: *Journal Asiatique*, *Anthropos*, *East and West*, *Numen*, *Temenos*, etc. He told me he would send them to New York and from there they would travel by ship to the homeland.

18 May

The day before yesterday, at 7:00 again, Folescu came with his wife. They went up and down on the library elevator three or four times, loading their car with all the offprints and magazines stored at the entrance to the attic, where Peter had carried them several months ago.

Today at 2:00 Folescu returned with a helper, Adrian. They carried away a hundred volumes (including Ibn Khaldun, the four-volume history of Greek philosophy by Guthrie, Friendländer's *Plato* in three volumes, etc.). Then they climbed the stairs to my apartment on

Woodlawn and filled several boxes (the collection of the journal *Antaios*, part of Jung's *Complete Works*, part of the *Eranos-Jahrbücher*, etc.).

I breathe a sigh of relief. Now I'm waiting for some sign from the library to which they are destined before shipping another eight hundred to one thousand volumes.

22 May

S. M. comes to see me. All she tells me about the cultural situation in the homeland depresses me terribly. And yet, although she could find work abroad, she will return to Romania. But she does not expect to be able to publish any "serious works." New directives from the regime forbid books of literary criticism or history which surpass two hundred pages, printed. "Economy . . . ."

24–26 May

I correct articles for the *Encyclopedia*; in the last few days I've received some six of seven pounds of them. And yet, I'm content with this work; I don't believe I could do anything *else*, anything more personal. For several days I've been struggling to finish my contribution to the article about androgeny, which Wendy O'Flaherty and I will sign together.

27 May

I try to gather together my working files for the summer.

NEW YORK, *30 May*

We arrived the day before yesterday, at 8:00 P.M. We left from O'Hare at 2:00, but on account of a heavy rain, we had to delay our landing in New York by an hour.

The rain continued all day yesterday and still hasn't stopped, even now. I read and corrected the package of texts for the *Encyclopedia* which I found here.

Last night we dined at Arthur Cohen's apartment, with three other friends of his. Thus I found again, for a few hours, the "atmosphere" in which I lived for many years (in former times): discussions about this, that, and everything, learned and vulgar allusions, memories of three continents.

1 June

The rain continued all day yesterday. Toward evening I finished correcting the articles. At 2:00 today Conyers and Beverly Moon came, and we worked together for almost three hours.

I didn't expect such hard labor when I accepted the post of editor in chief! Nevertheless, I don't regret it; the *Encyclopedia of Religion* will be *almost* as I envisioned it (at least in the sections I've supervised).

PARIS, *3 June*

The plane took off yesterday at 8:30 P.M., and we arrived here this morning at 9:00 Paris time. At the airport, waiting for us, were Giza, Dinu, Ileana Cuşa, and François Cochet.

5 June

In the envelope of mail forwarded from Chicago, several interesting letters: from Suhrkamp Verlag (newspaper clipping about the play by Pavel Kohut, *Auf der Mantuleasa Strasse*, which was performed at the Stadttheater in Bâle), from Mircea Handoca and Mac Ricketts (both asking what I believe about the "vital statistics" published, without comment, by Constantin Popescu-Cadem in *Revista de istorie şi teorie literară*, January-March 1983), and from Matthias Dalvit, a Swiss astrologist, requesting the exact day, hour, and minute of my birth, in order to be able to make my horoscope.

9 June

Finally, the first summer-like day. Since we came, cold and rainy. And yet, in spite of feeling tired (that seven hours' difference!), we've seen friends and acquaintances almost every day. Last evening, Eugène, Rodica, and Marie-France [Ionesco] came to our place for dinner (as usual, we recalled memories of youth!).

Today, Monica and Virgil came, with I. Negoitescu. Too many things to set down. I realize that the *Journal* has been transformed into a datebook. I write in it only late at night, in great haste and without enthusiasm. Nevertheless, I shall have to keep up the datebook properly speaking also; indispensable for the writing of *Autobiography* II (or III?).

11 June

In Chicago I collected a large number of notes and observations in an envelope, hoping I'd find time to copy them and integrate them into the *Journal*. This morning I discover among the file folders on the desk the notebook begun last year, which I had entitled *Notes for a Journal*. I leaf through it with melancholy: more than half the pages written are illegible to me now.

14 June

This evening, at Ionel and Marga Jianu's. Ionel has had some health problems, but he is resigned. We recalled, in connection with a recent visit from a fellow countryman, our first meeting in 1928—and we both found ourselves laughing heartily.

Last night we invited Monica and Virgil to our apartment, and we sat up talking until 2:00 A.M. Little by little we are finding out all that's happened in Romania and in the Romanian colony in Paris. Indeed, the day before yesterday, in the evening, with the Gomas and the Poghircs, we talked about almost nothing but Romanians and Romania.

15 June

We go to Virgil Tănase's place in order to see his wife and children. Impressed by all I see and all they tell me. In the evening we dine at Giza and Dinu's, with the Dehollains.

In the past six or seven days I've written numerous observations on large sheets of white paper. This time, I've forced myself to write legibly (something which isn't too easy, owing to my arthritis).

BORGO, 17 June

We left last night in a sleeping car; this morning we arrived in Pisa, where Vittorio Vettori and his wife were waiting for us. They took us by car directly to Borgo. We're staying in an old-fashioned but charming hotel with a garden, only a few hundred yards from the castle.

Toward evening we set out toward the castle; beside it is the seat of the Cassentinese Academy, of which Vettori is president. They have accorded me the Dante Alighieri Prize. Vittorio introduces me. Then an intelligent actor reads excerpts from the Italian translation of the *Journal*. I improvise a response of sorts, regretting sorely that I can't speak extemporaneously in Italian.

VERNA, *18 June*

Superb morning; clear sky and warm enough (last night we slept in an icy room, with three blankets over us). While we are waiting for the coffee in the garden, sitting on a bench in the sunlight, a *Cetonia aurata* wheels in flight above us. I find myself suddenly in the time of vacation, in adolescence, when I kept watch in the raspberry bushes . . . . *Cetonia aurata*, the coleoptera of greenish gold, which I never got tired of watching.

We ascend toward Verna. Hairpin turns, one after another. Hillsides covered with large clumps of broom and poppies.

We enter a forest. Leaving the car, we go on foot to the "sacred space": Verna, with the cave where St. Francis was embraced by a seraph and obtained the stigmata. We pause in front of the bed on which the saint slept. In order to "do our duty," we visit the basilica and several other chapels. Then we descend between the two walls of the mountain. Curious impression: I seemed to be breathing with difficulty, and yet I couldn't bear to leave . . . . No need to record any other details.

We return at 2:00 P.M. Vittorio's house (I believe he spent his youth here also): spacious, superbly furnished, complete with bookshelves, densely packed. Vittorio's mother (she is past eighty) prepares lunch for us.

BORGO, *19 June*

In the afternoon we start out for Camaldoli (which could mean, we are told, either *Campo amabile* or *Casa di Maldolo*). We ascend a steep road, through a forest, to the monastery (Cenobio). A superb library. But also a bookshop and large rooms for lectures. (And, of course, a hotel, several restaurants, cafés, etc.)

Then Vettori's car climbs higher, to eleven hundred meters, to Eremo San Romualdo. We see the saint's cell, but we can't go inside. Alongside, the *beata solitudine* of the Benedictines.

20 June

This morning Vittorio Vettori showed us Florence again, driving through it with much skill. We stop briefly in front of the churches and places which we wish to admire awhile. A little "adventure": the twelve- or thirteen-year-old boy begging at the door of a cathedral . . . . As I took out my billfold, the bills spilled and scattered on the pavement. We both began to pick them up. I saw the boy put his foot on a hundred-thousand-lire banknote, but I felt sorry for him—and I was ashamed—and I pretended not to have noticed. I gave him then a five-thousand-lire bill and started quickly toward Vettori—turning my back and allowing the little beggar to pull the banknote from under his foot.

We took the express at 3:00, and at 6:00 we were in Rome.

ROME, 20 June

We're staying at the Plaza, Via del Corso. In the early evening we visit briefly with Ruggiero Ruggieri, Piazza di Spagna, no. 3. One cannot imagine a house more "sensational" (the expression, I learned recently, is much used in tourist guidebooks). From the top floor the view is spectacular. But Ruggieri shows me the concrete fretwork directly in front; it camouflages, rather imperfectly, one of the numerous underground toilets ("toilets for the three sexes," someone has called them).

23 June

Yesterday morning I awoke singing *"Christos a înviat din morţi"* ["Christ has risen from the dead," an Orthodox Easter hymn].

I went for a walk alone on the familiar streets, but I didn't try to remember the years of my youth when I discovered them.

This afternoon, appointments: at 2:30 with Mario Bussagli; at 3:00 with Ferrari (we discussed again the project for a series of films for television: the life of the Buddha); at 6:30 with Sante Bagnoli, director of the Jaca Book publishing house: unexpectedly young and very likeable.

PARIS, *24 June*

On the 5:00 plane, but it was an hour late in taking off. We arrived in Paris at 8:00 P.M. I dreamed the whole time: I "saw" the subjects of several studies and a long novella. Too tired to record them here.

This time too our hotel was paid for by Italian Television—at Ferrari's request, of course. I'll have to "collaborate" on the scenario Ferrari is preparing with the advice and assistance of Bussagli. But—how?

25 June

I work as best I can on the *Autobiography*. I correct and transcribe several pages from chapter 20, written in great haste last winter at Palm Beach.

26 June

I realize now the great mistake I made: instead of "classifying" my correspondence for Regenstein's Special Collections, I ought to have worked on the pages of the *Autobiography* already written and continued chapter 20. But, I admit, I was fascinated—and paralyzed— by that disinterment of my past: those twenty-five years in Chicago.

28 June

Yesterday evening, along with the Ionescos and Cioran, we dined at Colette and Claude Gallimard's. I was bored, listless, finally depressed. General discussion: the talk was mostly about diseases.

Today I received by air express three books by Piero Scanziani. All with the same dedication: "To brother Mircea; brother Piero." I open

Libro Bianco at random; the text arrests me from the start and I read, fascinated, for several hours. What a joy to discover, at my age, a new writer!

29 June

Telephoning to invite them to dinner one evening next week, Christinel found out from Gaby that Jean Gouillard died two days ago.

An immense sadness. Last summer I did not see him. I remember about the beginnings of our friendship, in 1948–1949. How attentively and ably he corrected my manuscripts—many thousands of pages!

To me, he never seemed to age; I thought he was at least ten years younger than I. And yet, we learned from Gaby that he was seventy-four.

30 June

I write four pages for *Album Siegfried*, which Ionel Jianu is preparing (it will reproduce some of his latest watercolors, especially those from Venice). Four ordinary pages, which I have written with great difficulty, barely managing to hold the pen in my hand. I repeat to myself (in vain!) that I must learn shorthand, or at least how to type with one finger of my left hand!

1 July

I keep thinking about Jean Gouillard. I see him especially in my room in Hôtel de Suède, when he was still wearing a cassock. Yet another "contemporary" of our life—mine, Christinel's, and that of the Romanian exiles of the years between 1946 and 1956—who has gone.

Carmen and Ioan Culianu have arrived from Groningen.

2 July

This evening, at Paul Barbăneagră's. The Culianus took us in their car; talking all the while, we lost our way several times in that fascinating quarter, Le Marais, and we drove along place des Vosges, which I hadn't seen for several years.

Paul showed us his last film for television (about Athens). Some sequences admirable. But the text, at points, sets me thinking. The "decadence" of *classical* Greece disturbs me. We must have a long talk sometime. But when? And how—so that we understand each other? Paul is a visionary and a great artist. He hasn't had time to study the religious symbolism of cities, as analyzed, for example, by Paul Wheatley in his huge monograph *The Pilot*. Unfortunately, he doesn't know English. And he's not interested in the historical *realities* (see, for instance, Wheatley's book) whose symbolism he wishes to fathom.

3 July

At 11:30, in one of the salons of the Sorbonne, invited by Alfonse Dupront (together with E. Cioran and Eugène Ionesco—but Eugène is at Spoleto). Ceremony for the bestowing of the Ribbon of the Legion of Honor. In his long response, Dupront speaks about Cioran (actually, it was Dupront who saved him—by bringing him to Paris in 1938); after that he pronounces my name also. Following the ceremony, he squeezes both my hands, speaks to me with emotion (he wants to meet me again, to invite me to dinner, etc.).

Tired, dizzy (because I had a night of insomnia), but at 2:30 Culianu comes again, to take us in his car to Boulogne. An hour later we arrive at the church (name?). Five or six minutes later the body of Jean Gouillard is brought from the hospital. (In the meantime, C. Tacou and his wife have arrived; after almost two years we meet again. I whisper to Christinel that we must forgive him.) In the church, Gaby; to me she seemed drugged (too many sedatives), but perhaps she wasn't. A brief altercation with the priest when he begins the "service" in front of the coffin (the service was simplified to the maximum anyway). I didn't understand until at the end when N. Beldniceanu explained to me: Gaby is furious at the priest for refusing to accompany the bier to the cemetery. Jean had been *"le père* Gouillard"; then he had taken off his cassock and married. Owing to Père Laurent, however, he had not been excommunicated. But in the end, the "hierarchy" had triumphed.

4 July

Letter from Vettori: I have been accorded the Isola d'Elba Prize for "the best narrative published in Italian in 1983" (*Nozze in Cielo* [*Nuntă în cer]*, a novel written in 1938). The prize, four million lire, will be awarded in October, on the island of Elba.

My literary "career" outside Romania is full of surprises. Thanks to the success of the first German translation (*Pe strada Mântuleasa*), Siegfried Unseld decided to translate my whole literary *oeuvre* (so far, some eight or nine volumes have appeared). In Italy, the appearance of "the writer" Mircea Eliade caused surprise—but also interest, although Jaca Book is not well known as a literary publishing house. In the United States, little has been translated and, except for the *Autobiography*, without very great success (although *The Forbidden Forest* has gradually found its readers and admirers). But I don't understand what has happened in France, where plenty of my literary works have been translated. It's true, they have been published by Gallimard—and copies sent to critics were accompanied by that well-known insert: *Hommage de l'author, absent de Paris*.

6 July

I have put off recording what Ioana Miereanu said to me several weeks ago about the conception of life after death which she discovered recently in the village of her parents, in the Gorj district of Romania. For the past several years Ioana has been spending a part of the summer in that region, recording the songs, verses, and beliefs—especially those having to do with witchcraft and death. I had imagined that, after forty years of "socialism," the belief in the power of witches, like all other "superstitions," would have disappeared. I was wrong; at least in the region studied by Ioana, magical rituals and concepts are more alive than ever. What interested me most was the *creativity* of magico-religious folklore. It does not simply *repeat* the rites and beliefs that were flourishing fifty or sixty years ago, such as I knew in my childhood and youth. It articulates, for example, a new mythology of death and a new system of funerary rites, hard to imagine a half century ago. No longer is it a matter of services and feasts held for the repose of the souls of those "whom God has called" (as they used to say). Now people ask the priest (for pay, in money or goods) to celebrate certain services and recite prayers for their post-mortem "situation": namely, not only for the peace of their soul, but also for its *comfort* in the world beyond. Each person is forced to build there his own *house*. He "constructs" it by stages: the first services and feasts are for the walls, then others for the windows, the floor, the bed, the furniture (specifying the number of chairs, etc.). The people project, in a magical way, their *true* dwelling place (i.e., their *property*) in the existence which they will enjoy after death.

I urged Ioana to write up and publish as soon as possible this new mythology of death. It is, however we may be disposed to judge it, a new spiritual creation of the folk.

10 July

This evening, for dinner, we invited the director of Jaca Book, Sante Bagnoli, and his assistant, Maretta. Afterwards, they came up to our apartment, and we talked for almost two hours. I learn many things about the cultural situation in Italy. What impresses me most: the translation of the writings of Henry de Lubac in forty volumes and those of Hans von Balthaser in sixty-five volumes. It's as if we were living a half century ago. Jaca Book has planned its editorial program for the next ten to fifteen years.

As for their publication of collections of art, archeology, and sociology—their courage amazes me. It's true, the distribution of these expensive books is not through bookstores, but directly from publisher to reader, via the post office. And a good share of the volumes on the history of art, containing a large number of colored illustrations, are printed in Yugoslavia.

1 August

I finish (Finally!) writing and transcribing the preface (short and mediocre) for the excellent volume of Culianu, *Expériences de l'extase*. Jean-Luc Pidoux-Payot asked me for this preface as the *sine qua non* of his publishing the book; it was a matter of Ioan's first work in France, so it had to be "recommended by an authority." Since I kept postponing it, he sent the book to the press and reserved two pages for me. Then recently he set a "deadline": 20 August.

My admiration for Ioan is sincere and unlimited. But recently (when?—probably last winter) I realized that *any* deadline, *any* text which takes me away from the *Autobiography* reduces me to a larval state; I am incapable of thinking, even when I have no more than a few pages to write.

I hope I shall be able to write someday all that I think about Ioan Culianu.

August

I find the source of that admirable metaphor for death [in the Romanian language], *departe* (distant, far away). G. T. Kirileanu heard it from an old woman in Broșteni. She told him that, so far as she was concerned, "It's not long to far away"; that is, she hasn't much longer to live (*Corespondență*, 51). I wonder if anyone has studied the origin and diffusion of this expression.

I'm sorry now that twenty years ago I didn't encourage one of my students to carry further my observations relative to the "philosophical" importance of the cult of the dead. Actually, it was this cult that established the idea of the autonomy of the spirit.

A parallel with the situation of today: theologies have lost their importance and timeliness, but parapsychology and spiritualism "demonstrate," in the eyes of many, the autonomy and survival of the soul.

15 August

Somewhat melancholy, I finish reading the last volume of Ernst Jünger's journal: *Soixante-dix s'efface: 1965–1979*. It seemed to me rather didactic and prolix. So many trips: to Asia, Iceland, Portugal, etc., etc.—and all described in detail. Saddened especially by the uniformity of all the cities in the world. That wasn't true thirty years ago. Not to mention Egypt, Ceylon, and India in the time of my youth, 1928–1931, when I knew them.

17 August

For ecology today, Constantin Noica writes somewhere, "the environment or the swamp is truer than the frog."

19 August

The mysterious memory and the tricks it can play on you . . . . Out of the many verses of Camoens's *Os Lusíadas* which I once knew, I realized today that I now remember no more than this fragment: "*E a piscosa Cizimbra.*" I believe I understand why: *piscosa* means "full of fishes, fishy." The word impressed me from the first time I read it. And I couldn't forget it. But—for what reason?

GRONINGEN, *23–26 August*

Invited by Ioan and Carmen Culianu, we are staying in their house at no. 60 Korreweg. (This time, to save us from having to climb stairs to the second floor, they have bought a large and comfortable bed and camouflaged it in the living room.) Superb days, which we spend "resting"—that is, without sightseeing trips and without recorded conversations. (That interview-book for the new series edited by Paul Goma at Albin Michel—a volume which ought to complement the one by Rocquet, concentrating on the writer.) We walk around the city only when we feel like it. And since this is vacation time, almost all the professors are gone somewhere. I meet only the Africanist Witte, whom I'm thinking of inviting to write the chapter on African religion for *Histoire* IV. Excellent impression.

The pure delight of not having a schedule, of not doing anything, of holding conversations on any and all subjects! There's just one thing I'd like to discover: the location of G. van der Leeuw's house and the park and the streets where he liked to walk.

PARIS, *8 September*

Visit to Alice Godel's apartment at no. 2 rue Mermoz. She shows me the desk at which I worked in Val d'Or. Books, albums, photographs. The constant presence of Roger Godel. Too melancholy to add other details.

13 September

Evening with the Poghircs, Alain Paruit, and Mălina. I learn much about university life in the Romanian Socialist Republic, and in Germany as well. (Poghirc is professor at the University of Bochum.) Thanks to the enthusiasm and energy of Poghirc, the Centre Roumain de Recherches has resumed activities.

14 September

I finish chapter 22 of the *Autobiography.* Have arrived in the narrative at the first years spent in Chicago. From here on I shall have to summarize, condense.

17 September

From 4:00 till 7:00, interview with Petru Cirdu, poet from Yugoslavia. Some important review (name?) wishes to devote an entire issue to me. He brings me a copy of *Yoga* in Serbo-Croatian. It is the sixth volume of mine published in that language.

24 September

Yesterday I began reading those several hundred typed pages: articles for the *Encyclopedia,* sent from New York. I am not always in accord with their authors, but if the documentation is correct and (as much as possible) complete, I give them my okay. I shall not read more than a small part of the pages of those sixteen volumes of the *Encyclopedia,* of course; I haven't the competence or the curiosity to judge, for example, the history of the Christian sects or the sociology of religious movements in China. I imagine that the Free Press (Macmillan) will preserve the entire archive; it will be possible to know later which texts passed through my hands and how I evaluated them.
(27 September to 5 October: transcribed from the pocket notebook.)

PISA, 27 September

Vittorio Vettori is waiting for us at the airport. He apologizes for being unable to find us a room anywhere but at the Hotel Pace.

Impossible for me to remember how this part of the city looked forty or fifty years ago. But all I saw from Vittorio's car window fascinated me. And yet, I regret that I've let so many years pass without our stopping in Pisa for two or three days at least.

In the evening we dine at the picturesque and excellent Da Bruno Restaurant with the Vettoris and friends of theirs. I try to evoke the emotions of a young Romanian student in the spring of 1927, finding himself suddenly in front of the tower. Then we speak about other things, and I realize that my memory has deceived me: the emotions which I evoked, I experienced a year later, in front of the tower, but in other circumstances.

28 September

This morning, two interviews (impossible to refuse Vettori!). At 12:00 Roberto Mussapi and his wife arrive by car from Milan. Roberto "represents" (he says it with a trace of irony) the Jaca Book publishing house. We eat lunch together; then . . . two more interviews! Fortunately, the reporters ask interesting questions. (I find out that one of them is working on his doctorate in art history.)

In the afternoon, the ceremony at the academy (organized by Vettori, of course). I am, for reasons I don't quite understand, being "celebrated." Vettori speaks first, then a young scholar who knows many of my books; the president gives me a medal, and I thank him as best I can, in a brash, simplified Italian.

Vettori returns to Florence; tomorrow morning he will have to leave for Sicily. We promise to see each other again as soon as we can.

Meanwhile, Nina Battali arrives from Rome, curious to visit the island of Elba. We three Romanians dine alone.

ELBA, *29 September*

This morning, from 10:00 to 12:00: interviews. I don't recognize myself any longer! In order not to offend Vittorio, *or* the men from the academy, *or* Jaca Book, I accepted all requests for interviews. But I never imagined there would be so many!

Finally, at the beginning of the afternoon, we leave in Mussapi's car for Piombino, in order to take the boat for Elba. Nina Battali is with us. We are speaking three languages at the same time, because Roberto prefers English and his wife French. Luckily, we discuss literature mainly (only now do I discover that Roberto Mussapi is an accomplished poet).

A banal crossing, because the sky is overcast and rain is threatening. We arrive at Elba in darkness. The port and the surroundings make a detestable impression. Roberto assures us that he'll never come back: the island is too sad, the port too forlorn, the street lamps too few and too pale.

Fortunately, the hotel, the Airone, new and superb, pacifies us: we can't believe our eyes when we go inside. Waiting for us are several members of the committee which is giving me the prize, and the owner of the hotel. (I learned later that he started out as a laborer.)

After dinner we all gather in a salon in order to decide the schedule for the next day—that is, basically, more interviews.

30 September

This morning, the interview with the young man sent by RAI. I seem to speak Italian worse than ever. (Useless to tell them—the young man and the others—that as soon as I'm forced to speak into a microphone, I can't concentrate and I fail to find the right words.)

This afternoon, two more interviews. A fine rain began to fall; the garden in front of the hotel had pleased me so much that I had hoped we could have our talk while strolling through it. But we had to shut ourselves up in one of the unoccupied rooms.

Toward evening we set out toward Martino in the car belonging to Alfredo Cattabiani, writer and journalist come from Rome in order to attend the ceremony. It was to have taken place in the famous Piazza di Martino, where a platform had been erected and some two hundred chairs set in rows. But in the meantime a thunderstorm broke loose. In that half-hour ride, ascending through the forest with the shape of the curves ahead barely discernible, I saw nothing but the pale shadows of a few villas now and then.

We dined in a picturesque restaurant, in a group of about a hundred guests. But the storm intensified, and it was raining bucketsful. One of the newspapermen from Rome didn't dare get out of his car and cross the few yards of the parking lot that separated him from the restaurant. He waited for almost an hour before one of the waiters saw him and took him an umbrella. But when he entered the dining room, he was wet to the skin. Although he seemed out of sorts, he tried, nevertheless, to be humorous: he began asking those around him what literary figure he resembled, as he wrung out the sleeves of his coat like a piece of laundry.

Sheltered by a gigantic umbrella, we left the restaurant and took refuge in a nearby church. There, beside the altar, the "reception" was improvised: a long table, covered with a dark cloth, beautifully decorated. Only seven of the twelve members of the committee were present. The president spoke, giving a short history of the Island of Elba Prize; then he handed me the check. I thanked him, repeating sentences I had planned during the time we were eating.

But the true surprise was the concert of flutes. At night, with a storm raging, in an old and beautiful church dimly lighted, the melodies seemed to come from a long-forgotten dream, dreamt in childhood.

The car passed slowly through the square, and we had time to look at the platform and the two hundred chairs, waiting in rows, in the rain. Then, when we were nearing the hotel, the storm suddenly ceased.

ROME, *1 October*

We left Elba shortly after noon. The port of Piombino was jammed with tourists. Cattabiani brings us to Rome in his car. Enthusiastic discussion—not just about literature. The rain has ended, but the sky remains overcast, leaden.

2 October

Some four or five interviews and articles have appeared already, but Ferrari, who comes to see me at the Hotel Plaza, tells me there will be others. (I wonder how *he* knows?)

3 October

Mario Bussagli comes with his son, who is passionately interested in medieval religious symbolism. We discuss the project, ''Gautama Buddha,'' which so much preoccupies Ferrari: at least ten programs of an hour each on Italian television.

4 October

Chilled, fighting a head cold, I remain all day in the room, reading. In the evening we invite friends (Nina, Nicola, Pufuleţ) to the Toto Restaurant. As usual, long discussion with Nicola; he has recently reread D'Annunzio's first books (poetry, novel, drama) and discovered many interesting things.

PARIS, 5 October

We arrived today, toward evening. I hope I'm over my cold. But the right ankle is more inflamed than ever, although I've done very little walking. (I record these details in the hope that they will be useful to the doctors I intend to consult in Chicago. They still have not decided if the inflammation is caused by rheumatoid arthritis, or if it's something else: tendinitis, for instance.)

7 October

Today I dined with Mac Ricketts, his wife, and Adriana Berger. Christinel stayed home, fighting a cold.

Mac has come to Paris for a week to see the hotels and apartments where we have lived, to walk through the neighborhoods which were ours thirty years ago. He hopes, also, to find additional ''documents''— letters, manuscripts, photographs—for the book he is writing.

9 October

From 2:00 til 4:00, with Gyora Novak. We had arranged this meeting by telephone from London (when I was in Paris) several weeks ago. A handsome man of about forty-five or fifty with an unusually charming manner. He shows me the plans and tells me all about the

"Bridge of Peace" which he is going to build in Jerusalem. Enthusiastic. He "dreamt" the project (a gigantic spiral rising a hundred meters in the air) in a second, I don't know how many years ago. Actually, it's not a spiral; I don't know how to describe it. It will be entirely of metal, and gilded. It will *incarnate* the sacrality of Jerusalem ("City of Peace"), not only for the believers (and disbelievers) of the three biblical religions, but for *anyone:* Buddhist, polytheist, "primitive," etc. When the Dalai Lama saw the plans two years ago in London, he took both Novak's hands in his and repeated twenty times, "you must do it!"

Novak asks me to compose several pages about the symbolism and function of this "Bridge of Peace." I accept, but I point out that I have been suspected and slandered by many in Israel. My name could serve as a pretext for those who would oppose the project. He tells me that he had found out about all these things, but that the men of science who support him have advised him to take no account of them.

I'm afraid that he is mistaken. I would be sorry, not so much for the resumption of the campaign against me, as for the discrediting of the project.

From 4:00 till 6:00, with Mac Ricketts. I don't know yet what "discoveries" he has made in connection with my life in Paris in the years 1945–1956.

10 October

Depressed after reading Marin Preda's book, *Cel mai uibit dintre pămînteni* [The best-loved of the earthlings]. I couldn't go to sleep, even after taking two Ansiolin tablets. I kept thinking of what I would have suffered had I remained in the homeland as professor and writer. If it hadn't been for that *felix culpa:* my adoration for Nae Ionescu and all the baleful consequences (in 1935–1940) of that relationship.

12 October

At the Sorbonne, in the Turgot Amphitheater. The inaugural session of the Centre Roumain des Recherches under the presidency of

Cicerone Poghirc. Standing room only. I feel bad, almost ill, with my hands sheathed in "anti-arthritis gloves," barely able to move, leaning on my cane. I ought to have been seated beside the president on the rostrum, but I didn't dare sit there: I'd have had to say a few words (as former president of the center), but I was afraid; I remembered the years 1948–1955. Ierunca's talk on Mircea Vulcănescu—simply excellent. I'd like to have added just those words—his last—which Mircea transmitted to those of us living in the West: "Don't avenge us!"

13 October

This afternoon, Barbăneagră and his team from the television station came to continue the film begun three or four years ago. From 5:00 till 7:00, with floodlights in my face and on both sides. I had to resign myself. I knew the answers to the questions, but I didn't always answer as I wanted. In any event, I said things I've repeated in many of my writings, but sometimes I said them without nuances, perhaps even rudely.

I write this page in order to make clear the following: (1) this television interview expressed my ideas only approximately; (2) the text could not be cited as a reference to my general "system" (the new, planetary humanism, based on the recent hermeneutics of the history of religions). I request my executors to take account of this "deposition."

14 October

Between 2:00 and 3:00 I go to the Hôtel Diamond in order to say good-bye to the Mac Rickettses, who are returning tomorrow to North Carolina. They arrived in Paris on 7 October. A more unsuitable moment could not have been found: Christinel sick, I convalescing from my cold in Rome; two acupuncture sessions; the inauguration of the Centre Roumain at the Sorbonne; guests for dinner; three hours with the television, etc. We had just one chance to dine together (at the Relais Normand). Fortunately, Adriana entertained them: she walked with them everywhere; she showed Mac the buildings, or at least the streets, where we lived. Mac came to the apartment one afternoon, and we talked for two hours. But I didn't succeed in answering his questions;

and as for the promised manuscripts, I gave him only photocopies of my first "literary compositions" from 1919!

I was too tired (from the acupuncture? the cold?) to try to find the cartons or file folders whose contents would have interested him.

17 October

We dine at Alice Godel's, with Andrée Chédide and her husband, and with Dr. Dolto-Marette, whom I see again after twenty-five years. I know only in part the "career" she has had since then (books, series of lectures on the radio and television, etc.). I remember with emotion our first meetings. What interested me then, especially, was the solution she had found: she was, on the one hand, a practicing Catholic; while, on the other, she accepted without reservation the theoretical constructions of Freud. Nevertheless, she had succeeded (or so it seemed to me) in reconciling these two spiritual positions: she had found "the solution." But for me it was impossible to understand it!

18 October

I finish correcting and transcribing the text about Liviu Rebreanu for which Mircea Zaciu asked me long ago. Actually, it's a long letter to Zaciu in which I try to relate several memories. I copy here the essential parts:

> *I didn't see Liviu Rebreanu very often, but I did have the good fortune to have a few lengthy conversations with him. I should like to evoke especially our conversation about "the art and methods of the novel" (as Mihail Sebastian liked to say). Sometimes the observations of the great writer seemed banal, owing in the first place to his simple sentences and limited vocabulary, but they were not, in fact. On the contrary, they revealed judgments, nuances, and intentions which frequently escaped the listeners. I remember, for example, what he said about the creative function of repeated transcriptions, which I understood after a discussion we had in 1934 or 1935. We all knew that the Maestru "wrote with great difficulty," that he "polished the style" when he recopied the manuscript of the*

novel for the second or third time. But for Rebreanu, the recopying of manuscripts belonged to the same process of creation which had begun with the "original vision" of the work and was continued with the construction of the first "general plan" and the first sentences actually written. It was not a matter of "polishing the style," but of the continuation of the writing of the novel. In the first or even the second versions, the novel was "imperfect" in the etymological sense of the word: that is, "unfinished."

The Maestru *liked* Întoarcerea din rai, *but he expressed regret that I hadn't finished it. "It's only the first volume of a trilogy," I told him, trying to excuse myself. "That's not what I mean," Liviu Rebreanu interrupted me, with a smile that was kindly and stern at the same time. "This first volume* is *unfinished! If you had copied it just once, you would have discovered many things you didn't know, things important for the meaning of the novel." He was right, of course.*

. . . I wish I could say more about the cultural value and social function of literature as Liviu Rebreanu conceived it. As he said once to Mihail Sebastian, a novel or a play is like a house: you work a great deal to erect it, but after that you live in it or rent it. In our case, however, a novel is like a field of grain: you harvest it, you sell the grain, and you're done! The next fall or spring, in order to have another harvest, you have to sow again.

We all knew the situation of the Romanian writer, but Rebreanu was constantly seeking "solutions." Among them, I remember the importance he accorded to public libraries (which could buy, directly from the publisher, half the initial edition) and to translations into languages of wide circulation. One of the last times we met (I believe it was in the winter of 1939–1940), I ventured to express my doubts concerning translations. No foreign publisher could "debut" an unknown author from a minor or marginal culture; with rare exceptions, the translation of a single book was in danger of passing unnoticed; even worse, an unknown literature makes an impact through the publication of many high-quality authors. "You, Mae-

stre," I dared to say, "would be better known abroad if, instead of by Perrin or Lanciano of Carabba, you had been published by Gallimard or Mondadori, and if, along with your works, some books of Sadoveanu, Camil Petrescu, Matei Caragiale, Blecher, and others had also been translated."

He admitted I was right. But how could we succeed in interesting those few foreign publishers of great prestige? "Perhaps we'll have some luck," I added, "the luck of the Danes, for example. Danish culture is known today throughout the world almost exclusively due to two authors: Hans Christian Andersen and Sören Kierkegaard."

20 October

Traditional "Eliade night" at Barbăneagră's. I believe the "tradition" was inaugurated twelve or thirteen years ago; about thirty or forty guests (Romanian friends, French colleagues, and film workers) whom I wanted to see again before our leaving for the U.S.A.

I'm very glad that in this way I can meet again with certain savants and writers scarcely glimpsed during the vacation time.

But this time my tiredness embarrasses me, I have to stay seated as much as possible on a chair or sofa, and those who approach me and speak aren't always the ones I'd prefer. From time to time I get up, lean on my cane, and make for a certain group. Sometimes I take someone (Antoine Faivre, Paul Goma, etc.) by the arm and drag him along with me.

We return home not very late, yet exhausted.

I didn't expect this final "initiatory ordeal"—the decrepitude of old age—but I must face up to it. I must continue my "work" (that is, what I was predestined to do), despite all the infirmities which are continually multiplying: loss of memory, worsening of the myopia, physical fatigue, arthritic pains, and above all the immense difficulty of writing legibly.

21 October

Madame Louis Renou comes to see us. (She had invited us several times to dinner or tea, but we were always obliged to refuse.) I see her again after thirty-eight years. We speak about Indian studies in France since the death of Louis Renou and Jean Filliozat. Terrible melancholy, the cause for which I pretend not to understand.

25 October

Last night we dined at the Mihnea Berindei's. He is a Turkish studies scholar and an exceptional "activist" in the ranks of the Romanian resistance in Paris. We have heard repeatedly in the past few years from Monica, Marie-France, and others, about the courage, imagination, and daring of Mihnea Berindei. But last night we had the chance to hear him talking about his studies.

How new and interesting his interpretation of the politics of the Ottoman Empire in its age of glory seemed to me!

27 October

This evening at Maison Roumaine, Monica speaks. Excellent presentation of the cultural terror in the R.S.R. As usual, a tremendous amount of data; you have the impression that Monica has read all the books and magazines in Romania, and has forgotten nothing.

CHICAGO, *2 November*

We arrived yesterday evening, both quite tired. I have succeeded, nonetheless, in going through several kilograms of printed papers (the majority, information from India, Africa, etc., and requests for contributions for the sick in Africa).

This morning we rediscover the blue sky and the light of autumn—but not also the enthusiasm of other times. Melancholy. In my office at Meadville many more kilograms of paper greet me: letters, journals, packages of books which I am unable to open; I am forced to appeal for help to the secretaries in the office across the hall. I wonder, with horror, how much longer I'll be able to hold this pencil in my hand.

3 November

We learn that Joe Kitagawa, following an operation, was so weak that he couldn't articulate a single word.

4 November

We saw Joe a little while ago, for twenty minutes. He was brought home (after two months in the hospital!) the day before yesterday. He doesn't look bad, but he is weak and speaks with difficulty, groping for the words—and his voice sounds like that of an old man.

6 November

I see Dr. Sorensen. He prescribes gold injections of fifty milligrams once per week, starting today. Until I "recover." But I don't understand very well what he means. Till I "recover" from what? The pains? (I don't have too many.) The mental weakness? What?

I walk with difficulty because my left ankle is inflamed. After he examines it, Dr. Sorensen informs me that it is tendinitis; it has nothing to do with the arthritis. For the time being, I musn't tire myself, etc. We shall see later what can be done.

Later. . . .

10 November

Surprise! Among the books waiting for me at Swift Hall, I find a translation of *Domnişoara Christina* into the Czech language (Odeon, 1984), and a book by Stanislaw Tokarski, *Eliade i Orient* (180 pages; Nauk: Polska Akademia, 1984). I think, with sadness, that no Romanian literary historian has ever written about this problem—although at least some of them would have been capable of doing so.

12 November

I like this expression of J. L. Borges: "*las buenas causas perdidas!*" [the good lost causes]. I like it because it can be taken in several ways.

14 November

In the administrative and secretarial office a few yards from my own office I discovered today a new face. He introduces himself: Gengales Chatterjee, from Calcutta. I tell him that fifty-four years ago I lived in the Bhowanipore sector, on Bakulbagan Road. Smiling mysteriously, he replies that he too has lived in Bhowanipore, and that he is a relative (distant) of Rabindranath Tagore.

As a character in my novella *Podul* says, "All sorts of things happen."

20 November

Almost every day, letters. And every page "costs" me, as we used to say in lycée.

Fortunately, I no longer conduct any courses or seminars. All my time is at my disposition. For correspondence with foreigners, one of Joe's students, Peter, assists me. He also corrects and types the texts for the *Encyclopedia*. In addition, he helps me classify the rest of the books in my library.

24 November

For the first time, I wake up with my right ankle quite stiff. I can walk only by holding to the walls. The pain keeps me in bed twenty-four hours. Christinel telephones Dr. Sorensen. If the attack doesn't cease, the doctor assures her, he will come the next morning and give me a shot of cortisone. Fortunately, in the morning the pain has passed. But although Dr. Sorensen recommended: "Rest, rest, rest!" I go to Swift Hall. I had many papers to sign. When I return, my muscles ache and the sole of my foot is swollen.

November

Actually, I should have integrated into the *Journal* the notebooks of notes and comments, and even some quotations (Oriental and "primitive" texts too little known); it would become a fascinating summa, although hard to read and perhaps, to some, pretentious.

If only I'd kept some of my work files, even though inadequately dated: I'd have enjoyed reading them ten or twenty years later, along with the entries in the *Journal* proper.

I'd have understood many things.

Abraham could not "understand" the meaning of the sacrifice of Isaac; it was, apparently, an infanticide, and nevertheless Abraham knew that Yahweh could not demand such a deed. The "sacrality" of the sacrifice of Isaac was camouflaged, not in the "profane," but in the negative embodied in a "crime." Compare with the contemporary situation: religious experience today is unrecognizable because it is camouflaged in its contrary, in aspirituality, antireligion, opacity, etc.

From her journal, I discover that Virginia Woolf was not fascinated by *Ulysses* (see *Diary of a Writer,* 46). A detail which ought to weigh heavily in the history of the modern novel.

Cosmic Christianity—where God and Jesus appear as peasants, etc. . . . The parallel tendency in theologians and groups which see in God an alter ego. See the article in *Cahier* 6, 1980.

"Les mythes modernes sont encore moins compris que les mythes anciens, quoique nous somme dévorés par les mythes. Les mythes nous pressent de toutes parts, ils servent à tout, ils expliquent tout." (Balzac, *La vieille fille.*) (Modern myths are even less understood than ancient myths, since we are devoured by myths. Myths press on us from all sides, they serve all, they explain all.)

"Le monde ne sera sauvé, s'il peut l'être, que par des *insoumis.* Sans eux, c'en serait fait de notre civilisation, de notre culture. . ." (Gide, *Journal,* 24 February 1946.) [The world will be saved, if it can be, only by the *insubordinate.* Without them, what would become of our civilization, our culture?]

How happy for Gide to believe, thirty years ago, that the insubordinate could resist the police of totalitarian states! And yet, he was right: there is no other solution.

The inimitable Goethe: "I've never allowed myself to use induction!"

"If any two creatures grew into one, they would do more than the world has done." (Browning, "The Flight of the Duchess.")

"Il [Victor Hugo] ne portait pas encore la barbe, mais on savait qu'il la porterait." (Eugène Ionesco, *Hugoliades,* 88.) [He did not yet wear a beard, but one knew that he would wear one.]

25 November

I see Joe for the third time. Progress is slow. He has to sleep—and he sleeps a great deal of the time. Toward evening he speaks with difficulty.

28 November

I learn that during the operation, Joe's heart stopped beating for several seconds.

1 December

I have neglected this journal chiefly in order to put the final touches to a chapter of the *Autobiography.*

I don't know if I've noted this detail or not: last summer I gave to Guilloux a new selection of essays: *Brancusi et les mythologies,* the editing of which will be done by Alain Paruit. Some seven or eight of the essays have been published in English. I don't dare translate them myself. Moreover, many of the older texts (some corrected and amplified) must be revised stylistically. I'm glad that Paruit has accepted this responsibility.

7 December

I can't tell what the results of the gold injections have been. My hands remain as "encysted" as ever, and *l'abaissement du niveau mental* seems to become increasingly more pronounced.

One the other hand, I work with ever-increasing difficulty. The library, twice ransacked, has become almost useless to me; I can't find any book anymore, I don't know if I gave it to some library (in Romania, to Meadville, to Regenstein) or to some former pupil. Or if it simply disappeared during my absence.

10 December

Last night, at the Palmer House, the ritual banquet of the famous American Academy of Religion: to commemorate the seventy-fifth anniversary of its founding. In the largest room, on the seventh floor, some eighty round tables with over six hundred guests. The president, Ray Hart, and his wife, Christinel and I, Chuck Long, Nathan Scott, and the oldest former president of the Society for Biblical Studies are seated on the platform. The dinner and the speeches by Hart and Chuck last almost two hours. Then, "Ritual Complex," a musical piece composed in my honor by Professor Frank Burch Brown: oboe, violin, cello, and piano. Finally, the short presentation by Chuck (a presentation which Joe Kitagawa was supposed to make) and the "unveiling" of the sculpture by Isamu Noguchi entitled *Eliade* (a new "endless column" constructed out of paper)—the gift (priceless!) given me by the sculptor and the AAR.

For the first time in its seventy-five-year history, the academy is honoring, publicly and officially, a religion scholar. Applause, etc. I was tired (it was past 10:30), and although I had prepared several pages, I improvised for some twenty minutes. With success, it seems (so everyone tells me)—although, to me, it seemed uninteresting. Applause, everyone stands.

We go to the eighth floor, then, for the reception organized by the president.

PALM BEACH, *25 December*

We arrived last night. Our hostess, Mrs. Extor, is waiting for us at the airport. At the Ocean Echo we find again our room upstairs where the ocean can be seen.

This morning we were awakened by the light: the sun was streaming through the blinds. Warm. The sky exceptionally blue. Last night I had a dream about the *Autobiography*. (Note, July 1985: Unfortunately, I didn't record it. Now I don't remember it at all.) The first long walk along the beach.

This evening, Lisette arrives from New York. We dine at the excellent Crab Restaurant, where Lydia had made reservations for us many days in advance. We return to the Ocean Echo at close to midnight, buffeted by the wind; we hadn't realized that it had begun blowing with so much force.

26 December

Last night it rained, but toward morning the sky cleared. I dreamed a dream relative to the introduction I have to write for the *Encyclopedia of Religion*. I remembered a lesson given twelve or thirteen years ago. (Note: unfortunately I did not summarize the dream, and, of course, I've forgotten it.)

From 11:00 till 1:30 I worked at a table in the garden. I began chapter 23 of the *Autobiography*. Wrote seven pages. (I hope when I come to transcribe it, I'll be able to decipher it readily!)

27 December

Yesterday afternoon, in our room, I wrote two more pages. I realize that they're written in haste, but I can't help it. The important thing is to "continue the story": the first years spent in Chicago. I shall make corrections and additions (probably they will be the most significant observations and commentaries) later, when I have carried the story down to 1967–1968.

This evening, we three invited Lydia to dinner. Lydia suggested a restaurant which is, at the same time, a cafeteria and delicatessen. I was unusually edgy, without understanding why.

I am writing these lines in the garden after a walk of only fifteen minutes, because I mustn't tire my right leg (the tendinitis which has been bothering me for several weeks). I wonder if I ought to record such physical miseries. But perhaps they'll be useful to me later. No matter how the "physiological miseries" of today may evolve, I *must* learn to live with them.

29 December

Day before yesterday, only two pages. Yesterday, almost five. The weather stays beautiful. I write—and read also—in the garden.

This morning, my first walk of a half hour on Middle Road. (What a role this street and others nearby have played in my life of the last four or five years! How many novellas have I composed mentally, how many problems of the last volume of *Histoire* have I pondered here? And it was on this same Middle Road that I found that piece of jewelry.) As usual, lizards darting across the sidewalk, frightened at the sound of footsteps. And the same flowers—red, yellow, blue— whose names I've long since forgotten. Several butterflies. Surprise: a coccinela! (It should make me sad to be recording this "discovery": a poor coccinela, in the corolla of a red flower. Probably the next generation will know, out of the millions of species, only flies, mosquitoes, the most ordinary butterflies, bees, and—I hope—a few coleoptera.)

PALM BEACH, *1 January 1985*

Rainy day. I resume work on chapter 23 of the *Autobiography*. I succeed in writing three pages, after correcting and transcribing some five or six.

Yesterday and the day before, listless. (Perhaps because I kept thinking all the time of the too many projects in which I'm engaged. Now, of all times, when my health is more fragile than ever!)

Last night, New Year's Eve party at Lydia's, with Mr. and Mrs. Vergotti, a widow, and Donald Blackwood (he was once an actor, now an old man—but very well bred and polite, like most homosexuals; he doesn't hide the fact, but lives with his friend in an apartment which, I hear, is luxurious and beautifully furnished).

We return to the Ocean Echo soon after 10:00 P.M. But Christinel and I sit up reading till midnight, in order to wish each other "Happy New Year!"

3 January

Yesterday Gyora Novak came, and we talked in the garden from 4:00 till 6:00. Actually, he did most of the talking, and that was interesting. He wants at all costs for me to write that historical-philosophical text about "The Gate of Jerusalem."

That evening we invited him and his wife Judy to the Family Restaurant. Both Christinel and I are delighted with our new friends. In the case of Gyora, you don't know which to admire most: his courage, imagination, or will. . . .

6 January

I work till it becomes dark. Transcribe twenty-two pages. On January 4 Novak came to see me again. It's become cold, but the sky is as blue as ever.

This evening I finish reading (again) "A Boring Story" by A. Chekhov. Exceptionally impressive. I fall asleep late.

7 January

We left Palm Beach at 2:00. We shall take the plane at 4:00. *Deo concedente* (as Jung liked to say), we shall be in Chicago at 6:00, local time.

CHICAGO, *8 January*

Snowing. In two hours, the campus disappears beneath a white blanket. I work little: correct and transcribe a few pages.

9 January

Our thirty-fifth anniversary. We shall celebrate it alone, just the two of us. I work a little—only a few pages.

10 January

Yesterday I remembered about our marriage of thirty-five years ago and about Stig Wikander, the Puechs, and the Dumézils. This morning I receive a letter, serene and sad, from Georges Dumézil. He informs me that Madeleine has had a sudden reduction in her red blood cell count and is receiving blood transfusions. He adds, "I haven't been working for the past several weeks, and I am afraid to realize that this leaves me completely indifferent"—!

15 January

I receive a circular letter: "Rewriting History: Life Reeked with Joy," put together by Andern Henriksson. He presents extracts from papers written by pupils in a course about the history of the West from the Middle Ages on. It is simply unbelievable! If I didn't know that the "works" cited were available to any investigator, I'd think it was all a joke. The ignorance is so appalling that it becomes "creatively hilarious." I wish to cite only a few passages, but the *embarras du choix* paralyzes me. I choose at random:

"During the Middle Ages, everyone was middle aged. Church and state were co-operatic. Middle Evil society was made up of monks, lords, and surfs. It is unfortunate that we do not have a medieval European laid out on a table before us, ready for dissection. After a revival of infantile commerce slowly creeped into Europe, marchants appeared.''

"In the 1400 hundreds most Englishmen were perpendicular. A class of yeowls arose. Finally, Europe caught the Black Death.''

"The plague also helped the emergence of the English language as the national language of England, France, and Italy.''

"The Reformation happened when German nobles resented the idea that tithes were going to Papal France or the Pope, thus enriching Catholic coiffures.''

"The Popes, of course, were usually Catholic.''

"The last Jesuit priest died in the 19th century.''

"Louis XIV became King of the Sun.''

"Vauban was the royal minister of flirtation.''

"The Enlightenment was a reasonable time. Voltaire wrote a book called *Candy* that got him into trouble with Frèderick the Great.''

"The French Revolution was accomplished before it happened. The revolution evolved through monarchial, republican, and totalitarian phases.''

"History, a record of things left behind by past generations, started in 1815.''

"Great Britain, the USA, and other European countrys had democratic leanings. The middle class was tired and needed a rest. The old order could see the lid holding down new ideas beginning to shake. Among the goals of the Chartists were universal suffrage and an anal parliament. Voting was to be done by ballad.''

"Culture fomented from Europe's tip to its top. Richard Strauss, who was violent but methodical like his wife made him, plunged into vicious and perverse plays. Dramatized were adventures in seduction and abortion. Music reeked with reality. Wagner was a master of music, and people did not forget his contribution. When he died they labeled his seat "historical." Other countries had their own artists. France had Chekhov.''

"World War I broke out around 1912–1914. Germany was on one side and France and Russia was on the other."

22 January

I finish writing chapter 22, "I Begin to Discover America." Rather long: some fifty pages of manuscript. But upon rereading it, it seems to me mediocre. I write without any "sparkle"; banal, repetitive, too few interesting observations. (It's true, I wanted to finish as soon as possible.)

24 January

Since night before last, ill; the result of indigestion. With great effort, I correct and rework several pages of chapter 22. The truth is that I write with so much difficulty that I sigh in exasperation every time I take up the pen. I think: this is what I have to show for three years of treatments with colloidal gold (I've had twenty-five hundred grams already)! Plus somnolence and fatigue, and, worse, a progressive decline in memory and in all my mental faculties.

1 February

Three days at Mitchell (formerly Billings) Hospital for a new checkup. Fortunately, Dr. Cohen assures me, it's nothing serious. The irregular heartbeat, he tells me, presents no danger. The analyses made (especially that of the echo cardiograph, when we saw and heard the muscles of the heart throbbing) are more than encouraging. I have the heart of a young man.

The fatigue? The somnolence? Of no importance, Dr. Cohen tells me. Another encouraging test: the X ray of the stomach (after I had swallowed two glasses of barium) no longer shows the gastric ulcers identified five or six years ago. My opinion: probably the suspicious fatigue from which I suffer is the consequence of the injections of gold.

9 February

I throw away some ten or twelve pounds of paper: correspondence with various contributors to the *Encyclopedia,* copies of certain articles, my notes and comments relative to the "work sessions."

Altogether, some twenty bulging file folders, plus five packets of articles.

And yet my office remains quite as chaotic and overcrowded with files. Sometimes I'm tempted to call Regenstein and ask them to come and cart it all away!

PALM BEACH, *19 February*

We arrived on Saturday the sixteenth, at nearly 10:00 P.M. Happy that we'll forget for a week the cold and troubles of Chicago.

The next day, Sunday, the sun awakens us. Almost 80°. Christinel telephones Carroll Owen and finds out that Dr. Gerald J. Strauss will see me the next day in his office at 2625 N. E. Fourteenth Avenue, Wilton Manors, some forty or fifty miles from Palm Beach. On Monday Carroll took us there in her car.

Too complicated to explain how we made the decision to come. Gyora Novak was concerned about my arthritis and the disastrous psychomental effects of the gold treatments. He made inquiries among his friends and acquaintances; he consulted especially Carroll, whose ''specialty'' is hard for me to define (I don't know enough about all she does).

Her advice: to consult Dr. Strauss, who has ''worked miracles'' with acupuncture (learned or perfected in China) and chiropractic. Christinel was convinced and I accepted the ''experiment'' because I wanted to escape the winter in Chicago.

Yesterday, 18 February, I met the famous ''healer,'' who, Carroll told us, had saved her life many years ago. (It was Carroll also who had informed Christinel by phone when I was in the hospital for the checkup that the gold treatment was disastrous for my mind—something I'd suspected.) Dr. Strauss won my confidence from the start. After he had read the report brought from Chicago (the results of the tests), he stuck six long needles into me: into my liver, spine, stomach, chest, and the back of my neck.

I am to see him again tomorrow. This time he will examine Christinel also.

On our way home, because we wanted to eat dinner in a picturesque restaurant, Carroll proposed d'Anjou in suburban Lake Worth. Excellent.

22 February

The weather has continued, until this evening, to be more beautiful than we imagined possible. We dined with Mary and Roger at d'Anjou. We returned an hour ago. I shall try to summarize the last three days.

Wednesday, Carroll took us to Dr. Strauss's. Another six needles, which he left in place for ten minutes. He tells me he is delighted with the results. The fluids that had accumulated—not only in the joints of my hands and fingers, as I believed, but also in my feet and certain internal regions—have diminished appreciably. I must drink eight to ten glasses of distilled water daily for several weeks. I must stop taking the gold shots. (I had decided this myself, and even Dr. Sorensen had interrupted the injections for a year, in order for me to see if the gold was the cause of my weakened state of the past several months . . . or if it was old age.) Dr. Sorensen had suggested treatment with prednisone–but Strauss is opposed to it.

I don't know how much he can help Christinel. He took some eight or ten X rays and prescribed a number of exercises for her! And, inevitably, the six needles—which provoked, the next day, sharp pains. But the day after that the pains ceased, and Christinel felt truly a general improvement in her physical condition.

Today, with Carroll, I went for a third time to Wilton Manors. Dr. Strauss gave up a trip just to be able to see me again. Once more, the six needles. Then, advice: twice a day I am to hold my hands in hot paraffin (something Dr. Sorensen suggested many years ago). Beyond that, he is very well satisfied. I'll keep in touch with him by telephone. I promised we'd return in April.

23 February

Gyora Novak came to see me at 5:00. He informed me of the "latest developments" in connection with his project, "The Gate." I promised him the text of the article (for which the *New York Review of Books* is waiting) in ten or twelve days—at least a provisional text, which could be improved after being read by several scholars and journalists. At 7:00 Judy Novak and Carroll arrived, and (for the third time in five days) we invited them all to d'Anjou in order to celebrate Gyora's birthday with Veuve Cliquot champagne and French wines. Actually, he and his wife had come from New York explicitly to see me and to talk about his dream— and mine (and that of tens of thousands of others): "The Gate."

24 February

This evening we dine at the Novaks' little apartment.

CHICAGO, 25 February

At the airport to which Carroll took us, we found out that the plane was an hour late.

We land at O'Hare at 7:00. Fortunately, Stelian is waiting for us.

I go to Meadville to see if Peter (who, in my absence, was to try to put the hundreds of folders, boxes, and cartons in my office into good order) had found the typed copy of the five or six chapters of *Autobiography* II and, especially, the original text of *Fragments d'un journal* I, which I had put together after L. Bădescu informed me that he had burned up the two typed copies I had given him.

He has found nothing. My last hope: that Adriana sent the *Journal* fragments to Regenstein Library.

27 February

Yesterday evening we ate dinner with K. and Edward Levi at the Hunan Restaurant. I talk with them briefly but enthusiastically about the project, "The Gate."

Today, questioned if she knows anything about the Romanian text of the *Journal,* Adriana comes to my office and promptly locates the whole package.

Finally, something to be happy about! But discouragement settles on me again, as I realize I can scarcely write. . . . I must learn to dictate!

8 March

We invite Evelyn and Joe Kitagawa to a restaurant in order to celebrate our birthdays (the eighth and ninth of March, respectively).

It's Joe's first "outing" since last August. I try not to let myself become downcast. As usual in the evenings, Joe is tired.

9 March

Alexandra and Saul Bellow invite us to T. J.'s Restaurant—our favorite for two years—to celebrate my birthday. Melancholy. I keep thinking of Joe.

14 March

I write less and less often in the *Journal*. (And I no longer succeed in keeping up the *Datebook,* recording at least the most significant meetings with people.)

Never have I known such a period of sterility, fatigue, and detachment from that which—up till now—meant my "life and work." It is true, writing tortures me (pains in the joints of my right hand whenever the word is too long!). When I have no desire to work, I read whatever I happen to see: books of philosophy, Romanian reviews, novels, etc. Fortunately, I've corrected dozens of texts for the *Encyclopedia* (they send me packages every other week). I feel I'm doing my duty as editor in chief, that I'm not just wasting my time.

16 March

Yesterday I didn't have the time (or the disposition) to continue the description of my present "situation." I have the impression that the last treatment (without colloidal gold) or else the experiment with the acupuncture at Wilton Manors has provoked a negative reaction. In the first place, a "derangement" and sudden decline of mental faculties (a blockage whenever I'm seeking the "right word" or the name of an author I want to quote or the title of a famous book, etc.). But, on the other hand, this *abaissement du niveau mental* could be caused by a process accelerated by senility, which I didn't expect. I tire quickly, even (or perhaps especially) physically. I breathe hard after climbing the stairs to our apartment on Woodlawn Avenue. It's been perhaps two months since I've walked on the streets more than ten or twelve minutes at at time (from home to Swift Hall).

20 March

Now that I've begun, I must continue. The worst problem: the chaos my papers are in (the *Journal* notebooks, manuscripts, correspondence, files with notes, little boxes with studies and articles about me). If I should be suddenly incapacitated, no one would know *what I had in mind to do* with them, which materials were to be sent to Regenstein, which to place Charles Dullin, which to Culianu, to the American Romanian Academy (Professor Manea-Manoliu). I shall have to explain—but how? to whom? I tell myself that, with a little luck, I'll get over this spell and will begin by sending the Romanian books (some three to four hundred—the rest I've already given to Regenstein Library) to the headquarters of the ARA. The second phase: the donation of several hundred other volumes to the Meadville library, where they will remain easily accessible to me and where there's no chance of their being stolen (as at Regenstein).

In any event, before our leaving, I must send to Paris all *my* books, in various editions and translations, as well as certain manuscripts, the *Journal,* and a part of the correspondence. Probably I'll take the *Journal* with me; I need it for continuing the *Autobiography.*

WASHINGTON, *15 April*

Alf Hiltebeitel and Diana Apostolos-Cappadona meet us at the airport to take us to George Washington University. We have a reservation at the River Inn, a spacious room with a kitchenette. In the evening, at my request, we are left alone. We eat dinner at the hotel restaurant, then go upstairs to our room and to bed. Both very tired.

16 April

Surprise: blooming trees, tulips, and late spring flowers in every courtyard.

This afternoon, the president of the university, Lloyd Hartman Elliott, comes to meet me, accompanied by the chairman of the Religious Studies Department and two other professors. Discussion (fortunately, I feel in "good form") from 4:00 till 5:00. In the evening we dine with Alf, together with Professor and Mrs. Nasr and my former student Charles White. Nasr tells us how he escaped from Teheran. He asks me if I have received the Persian translation of *The Sacred and the Profane,* recently published (I haven't). Other translations have been announced, Nasr adds. He promises to keep me "up to date."

It is nearly midnight when we return to the River Inn.

17 April

Superb day. The sky is bluer than in Chicago.

Alf comes to the hotel at 3:30 to find out what's been happening in Swift Hall and how the program in history of religions is evolving. He is troubled by the fact that Wendy, so learned and brilliant, doesn't take "the sacred" seriously.

At 4:00 Diana takes us in her car to the university. Almost two hours of discussion—questions and answers—with members of the course taught by Alf and Diana plus three other professors (of anthropology, philosophy, and art) in the past winter and spring, "Mircea Eliade, History of Religions and the Artist." Although I don't make myself ludicrous, I am not "in form": I grope for words, etc.

At 5:45 I feel suddenly very tired, and I bring the discussion to an end. I realize once again that I'm no longer capable of "discussing" as I used to be. I knew (instinctively!—as Father used to say) why I refuse invitations to hold lectures and discussions, and why I hesitated so long before accepting Alf Hiltebeitel's invitation. Very probably the lecture tomorrow ("*Homo Faber* and *Homo Religiosus*") will be my swan song. After fifty-five years of lectures improvised in Romanian, French, and English—that's not so bad!

18 April

The ceremony went better than I'd expected. Diana came and took us at 7:00. At the university I meet again the president, the department chairman, and the other professors I had met the day before, plus several others. I don don my robe and we enter in procession, some thirteen or fourteen of us, with the president in front, into the small auditorium, three-quarters filled. The title of *doctor honoris causa* in humanities is conferred upon me. The text read by the president—almost superlative. Presentations—short, but very laudatory. I begin reading my lecture at 8:00 and finish the reading at 8:55. The applause lasts several minutes.

We withdraw from the podium and cross the auditorium in procession. Again, I feel tired (I had stood too long, had spoken for almost an hour). I try to rest on a bench, but several members of the audience approach, congratulate me, and ask questions. A car takes us to the University Club, where a reception is being held (cheese, fruit, white wine, etc.). I succeed in resting my voice with Diana and another young professor standing guard over me.

From all sides, praises. A shame that I can't let myself get involved in discussions.

I see Razi and his wife again, after some fifteen or twenty years. We finish the evening at their place, in Georgetown, where we visited them in the winter of 1957. We had come to Washington and were guests of Richman, who had invited me to give a lecture at his center (impossible for me to remember the name of the institute he had created and was in charge of).

And so, as I had decided, the swan song. I am content.

19 April

The sky is still just as blue, but to me the heat seems abnormal: 90°!

We visit the Phillips Art Museum, "guided" by Arthur Smith. I hope I'll be able to have a more leisurely conversation with this Arthur Smith: artist, painter, and professor of art history at the university. Unlike other faculty members—Alf and the professors of philosophy and anthropology—Smith speaks perfect French and (at least, so he says) has read, in Paris, all my literary writings.

We meet at 4:00 to continue our conversation. But after two hours I begin to feel tired and return to the hotel. We both hope we'll be luckier next time.

20 April

At 3:00, short visit with John Nef; he fell in the bath recently and broke his arm; taken to the hospital, he had surgery, but an infection set in, which he is still fighting. He came home only yesterday evening.

Evelyn—young, radiant. She attended Chagall's funeral. When John enters the room, supported by both arms of the valet whom he has hired since the accident, scarcely moving his feet—tears come to my eyes. In vain do we talk about "his immense *oeuvre*" and other things.

The "program" begins at 4:00. In a room with sofas and chairs, with tables and stands, we will remain almost seven hours. Fortunately, Christinel didn't come from the beginning, because until almost 6:00 I answered questions asked by students and professors. Charlotte and Nathan Scott have arrived from Charlottesville for this reception (three hours by automobile—and they have to be back home by midnight), and Chuck Long arrived by plane. Present also were more former students of mine: Norman Girardot (fearful for the fate of the history of religions in the U.S. after I no longer am alive), Mac Ricketts (who brings me his translation of the latest chapters of the *Autobiography*), Charles White, and several others. It was past 11:00, and I couldn't bear to leave. I knew it was, indeed, my "swan song," my last public lecture followed by discussion. . . .

I have written these pages lest I be tempted by insomnia.

NEW YORK, *21 April*

Diana, the Hiltebeitals, and the Girardots accompanied us to the airport. I feel quite tired, but I keep telling myself that I'm past seventy-eight, and at such an age. . . .

22 April

Conyers and Beverly Moon come to see me at the beginning of the afternoon. The *Encyclopedia* must appear in December 1986. The last deadline for late articles: December 1985. (And I have yet to write an introduction of about ten pages, typed.)

CHICAGO, *24 April*

Yesterday, from 5:00 till 8:00 P.M., I worked on the *Journal* for 1949, trying to establish the Romanian text according to the original notebooks and several fragments published in reviews. It took me *five* hours to put the finishing touches to a few pages! Today, I went over the work. Two hours have passed, and I'm exhausted, exasperated. I have the impression that I'll never finish! And I believe I've already devoted at least sixty or seventy hours to this task!

All this because poor Lucian Bădescu believed that his translation would take the place of the original if he destroyed those two typed copies.

30 April

I've been obliged to continue with this idiotic work, as much as four or five hours per day. I succeed, thus, in "wrapping up" a few pages. But more often than not, the next morning I discover I've forgotten something, or else (more stupidly) that I've copied, with enormous difficulty, pages already transcribed by Adriana or contained in the original manuscript (not the notebooks themselves, but the selection I made fifteen years ago for Christinel to type).

1 May

I don't mean to complain, but this is how it is: although I spend at least six or seven hours per day in the office, *I don't do anything!* That is, each day I begin a *different* "work in progress" without ever finishing any of those works. One day the chapter on Hinduism for *Histoire* IV; the next day, the chapter about Australian religions; the third, I reread a good part of my Romanian-language articles (1945–1965) and begin selecting and correcting them, with a view to the edition of which C. Poghirc spoke to me last summer. . . .And every evening, at home, I try (and sometimes I succeed) to read and evaluate *circa* forty to fifty typed pages of material for the *Encyclopedia of Religion.*

If I should be suddenly incapacitated, no one could make heads or tails of the chaos in my office. Sometimes this thought terrorizes me. I tell myself that I *must* gather up the various notebooks of the *Journal,* classify at least some of the manuscripts, specify which are to remain at Regenstein, etc.

3 May

I haven't recorded our "dinners out" at restaurants (T. J.'s, Hunan) with the Bellows, the Edward Levis, François Furet, etc.

Surprise: a letter from Pericle Martinescu (whom I haven't seen in almost fifty years) and his book of memoirs, in which he has included the interview with Mircea Handoca. I read it, of course, the same evening. He evokes our youth, the years 1932–1939, with an exceptional memory. I'd not forgotten that tremendous era, but I hadn't thought about it for a very long time. . . .

9 May

A few days ago the dean, Chris Gamwell, telephoned me, asking if he could come to see me. He gives me this news (which I must keep secret until 30 May): the president, the trustees, and the senate of the university have decided unanimously to create the Mircea Eliade Chair for the History of Religions. In this way, I shall continue to be present at the University of Chicago. He points out that this is the first time that a professor emeritus has been "honored" in this way.

I admit that this news has pleased both Christinel and me greatly.

10 May

This evening, a reception and banquet at the Quadrangle Club, preceded by two lectures in Swift Hall, commemorating the ten years of Joe Kitagawa's deanship of the Divinity School (1970–1980).

At the banquet, several speeches and toasts. Chris G. had asked me to speak also: a toast of two or three minutes. I had prepared a text in which I evoked our friendship. In vain. As usual, I improvised; I hardly had time to recall our first meeting at Ascona in the summer of 1955.

I was on the Dean's left, while Joe was on his right, next to Evelyn. He said something to me (thanks?), but I couldn't understand him.

Already eight months have passed since the fatal operation (the second one, when his heart stopped for several seconds), and his recovery of language proceeds slowly still.

13 May

I try to convince myself that I *don't have* too much to do before becoming *completely free*—that is, before finishing my "work." Indeed, what do I *have* to write?

(1) Two chapters (Oceania, Hinduism) and the final chapter of *Histoire* IV: about 100 to 110 pages, typed.

(2) Three articles (about 40 to 50 pages of typing) and the introduction (10 pages) for the *Encyclopedia*.

(3) Volume 2 of the *Autobiography*. I can't estimate the number of pages.

I believe there are about one hundred fifty typed pages representing the years 1938 to 1958. I'd like to be able to "narrate" as briefly as possible the events of my life between 1958 and 1977. I could add, then, in a short epilogue, the works, the "honors" I've received, and the organization of the *Encyclopedia* for the years 1977–1985. But even if I don't succeed in completing *Autobiography* II, I'd like to write at least a part of my "American experiences" and summarize my beliefs and ideas in "venerable maturity."

With a little luck (and my whole life has unfolded under a good-luck sign!), I'll perhaps succeed. But I struggle against obstacles unanticipated until a few years ago: I write with difficulty, I feel "detached" from my oeuvre, and, especially, I waste time on trifles (the reworking of the *Journal,* giving away books, the problems raised by the immense quantity of correspondence with Romanians and others). What am I going to do with those boxes? Give them all to Regenstein Library? But the letters received from Romanians in the last twenty-five years, so precious for understanding the Romanian diaspora, can be of interest only to us Romanians.

15 May

I reread the last three pages. How simple it would be if we had had *heirs,* if Sibylle had lived, or Ioan Cuşa. . . .

BOULDER, COLORADO, *18 May*

We arrived yesterday afternoon. Staying at the Hilton Hotel. We invite Davíd Carrasco, Jane Swanberg, and their two friends to eat dinner with us.

Today at 12:00 noon, some of the members of the Eliade seminar are guests of Professor Senesh (of the Academy of Independent Scholars) at his splendid house in the forest. After lunch, an hour of discussion relative to *The Old Man and the Bureaucrats* (*Pe strada Mântuleasa*). Then we all go to the university for the "ceremony." I want to preserve here the program, especially for the title: "Reception for Mircea and Christinel Eliade." Music (Handel, Bach, etc.), followed by a short introduction by Davíd, a reading from *The Old Man* by Jane, and Romanian dances performed by the daughters of Professor and Mrs. Mircea Fotino. I listen also to excerpts from the studies which three professors, members of the Eliade seminar, have devoted to me.

Davíd presents us with a copy of the book *Waiting for the Dawn: Mircea Eliade in Perspective,* a volume prepared and edited by Davíd Carrasco and Jane Swanberg. Only now do I have a chance to look at it and leaf through it. Excerpts from my writings and three papers by members of the seminar, plus many, many photographs. For nearly an hour I sign copies bought by "fans."

This evening Christinel and I dine at Ingrid and Mircea Fotino's.

19 May

Meetings and discussions. The weather is gloomy, and in the evening rain begins to fall. Davíd had planned dinner at a famous restaurant in the mountains, an hour's drive from here. But he is afraid to go because, there, snow has begun to fall. We dine, instead, with a group at a French restaurant. Tomorrow we leave.

CHICAGO, *21 May*

I receive the "official letter" from the president of the University, Hanna Gray. It is worth reproducing:

Dear Mr. Eliade:

I have the privilege of informing you that the University's Board of Trustees has formally established a new chair in your honor, to be designated as the Mircea Eliade Professorship in the History of Religions.

We are all delighted with this action. It is taken in recognition of your exceptional contribution to the world of scholarship and of the distinction you have brought to this University.

With every best wish,

Cordially,
Hanna Holborn Gray

22 May

I regret that in one of my last lessons last year, when we were speaking of Docetism, and especially of the temptation of Docetism to which so many Christian asceticisms and fanaticisms succumb (the disgust, the almost pathological horror of the body—in spite of belief in the Incarnation)—I regret that I didn't remind the students of this passage of André Gide's *Journal* (24 April 1907): "Mme. de Watteville. Grande 'distinction' morale. Mais croit un peu trop que les vrais poètes ne vont jamais aux cabinets." [Madame de Watteville. Great moral "distinction." But she believes a little too much that true poets never go to the toilet.]

25 May

Since last year I have given to Larry Sullivan almost all of my books on South American religions. To Bruce Lincoln I've given a mere ten volumes about Indo-Europeans, but I've promised him the rest (especially the complete works of Dumézil, plus Wikander, C. Devoto, Bosh-Gempera, and others). Sanskrit texts and Indianistics to Wendy O'Flaherty, *Barabudur* and other works about Buddhism to Frank Reynolds. But how many other hundreds and hundreds of precious books remain to be divided among former students and current colleagues! This before giving what remains (and there will be plenty remaining!) to the Regenstein and Meadville libraries.

I don't quite understand why I felt the need to write this note. It would have been more useful for me to make a list of the persons I'm thinking of [giving books to]. But such exercises depress me quickly, and I prefer to put them off till another day.

31 May

Yesterday, from 4:30 till 5:30, a "reception" in my honor. Larry Sullivan and Frank Reynolds speak.

At 7:00, dinner. During dessert, Bob Grant and Wendy O'Flaherty give talks; then a rather lengthy and picturesque speech by Jerry Brauer about the "mishaps" surrounding my establishment at the University of Chicago. I found out that the person who donated the million dollars (and who wishes to remain anonymous) has insisted that a *new* chair in the history of religions be created bearing my name. I had thought at first that the university senate had decided to name the chair I had occupied for almost thirty years, for me.

1 June

For several weeks my time has been preempted by work on the *Encyclopedia* and preparation of the Romanian text of *Fragments d'un journal* I. I have completed, finally, the compilation on shamanism, the long article for the *Encyclopedia*. On May 31 we dined at Dr. Sabău's home, located some twenty miles from Chicago.

The art fair has opened. I content myself with looking at a dozen or two "representative" works: paintings, jewelry, fabrics, ribbons. I remember how curious I was, examining this exhibit in our first year in Chicago. But I'm tired, in low spirits; actually, I'm sick: rheumatoid arthritis, or just the consequences of the treatments with gold. And I still have so many things to do before our departure. . .

11 June

Yesterday afternoon, interview with Kenneth Woodward from *Newsweek* magazine. Martin Marty is present too. I can't tell how bad I was; at any rate, mediocre. Especially since I saw the recording apparatus on the desk beside me. I'd have refused this interview if Marty hadn't informed me that Woodward had read several of my books and was *really* interested.

Again today I had to make conversation (another interview, this time for a first-rate Yugoslavian magazine) with the Indianist, Milita— Wendy's pupil. This time the conversation interested me. I found out, among other things, that the Serbo-Croatian translation of *Yoga*— handsomely printed—has had great success and will appear soon in a new edition.

14 June

All the plans for shipping my manuscripts, articles, etc., to Paris have been dropped. I have been content to gather together the majority of my own books and entrust them to Folescu, to be sent to Paris by air mail. I've succeeded in selecting also a few file folders, materials I'll need this summer in Paris. The ten or twelve *Journal* notebooks I'll take with me.

I realize that to send the entire archive (not to mention the 90% of the correspondence given to the library) would require several weeks of work on my part; I hope I'll be able to do it this fall.

15 June

The whole day at the office, trying to put it into some kind of order. I succeeded only in clearing the desk and putting together several files which Peter will mail to me.

PARIS, *21 June*

Both of us are still sleepy and tired.

Yesterday Ierunca and Dinu Noica came, accompanied by Dinu's niece, Simina, at whose place he's staying. We discussed nothing but the problem of the publication of the French translaton of Lucian Blaga. Dinu has discovered the originality—and the novelty and *timeliness*—of Blaga's thought. He selected texts from the principal works (in Romania) and obtained the right to bring the manuscript (four hundred fifty typed pages) out of the country. I promised him long ago, in a letter, to find a publisher. I shall apply first to Jean-Luc Pidoux-Payot.

I hardly spoke with Ierunca. Dinu, it seems, is depressed about what is happening in Romania, and he is afraid that Romanian culture itself will be obliterated.

June

The square in front of our windows is beginning to disappear. The workmen have broken up the cement and pulled up the sidewalk. Today it looks as if it had been bombed: shattered in pieces. I hear a man saying that place Charles Dullin will become "the most beautiful square in the Eighteenth Arrondissement." "No, no!" the old man with whom he is speaking corrects him. "It will be the most beautiful square in Paris!"

I repeat these words over and over to myself, in order to drown out the noise of the pickaxes and drills the workers are using to break up the cement in Charles Dullin Square.

28 June

Yesterday evening, an incredible adventure (incredible for me, at least, who believed that, at seventy-eight, I'd learned how to protect myself). . . . Last year I was invited by a Professor Chris Vidal to a session of the Dasypeltis Circle, for a "*soirée en l'honneur de Mircea Eliade.*" I excused myself as best I could, but I made the mistake of promising to come the next year. I believed it was a group of young writers and artists who would have a discussion, to which I would add a few observations.

A few days ago I received an invitation to the "Forty-first Session of the Dasypeltis Circle," Café de Flore, second floor. A little printed invitation on colored paper, with a unicorn design, announcing that I was to be "honored." The invitation under the sign of the unicorn reassured me somewhat: it was a matter, surely, of a small, private circle. I wouldn't risk finding the place crowded with "admirers" and the curious.

Indeed, I found it almost empty. After a few minutes, a short young man with an abundant beard approached me: Monsieur Vidal. He seated me at a table between two couples whose names I didn't catch. Professors, certainly, or researchers or artists. At the other tables, situated close together along the wall, some fifteen or twenty other young—and not so young—people. I looked at them in a friendly way, and the majority smiled back at me. Time passed. The waiter kept bringing coffee, mineral water, beer, and even a few glasses of milk, which the customers paid for on the spot. I asked for a Badoit.

After the waiter left, Monsieur Vidal got to his feet and, addressing me, asked me to speak to them about "the steps of my intellectual formation." I managed to control myself, but the first sentences were rather harsh. I had expected a dialogue, I told them. Nevertheless, I continued. I told them about my activity in the U.S. (the University of Chicago, our journal *History of Religions,* the *Encyclopedia*). Several rather ordinary questions—but the same old thing. Pretexts to take up again the "problem of India," of Aurobindo, etc.

After an hour, in order not to lose my temper, I stood up, confessing that I was tired, that I was still oriented to American time (seven hours' difference). Monsieur Vidal escorted me to the head of the stairs. . . . In the fall they will publish a review which will contain my "article." Of course, I refused permission, but I don't believe I dissuaded him.

Going downstairs alone, I found myself in the milieu which I had not seen in a long time: the lights of the cafés Le Flore and Les Deux Magots: the tables crowded together on the sidewalks, the groups of tourists looking around excitedly. . . . Too many memories all of a sudden. Melancholy. Fortunately, I remembered what I had recently discovered: that *dasypeltis* is the name of a snake of East Africa. But I regretted that I didn't know more: why they had chosen this as the name of their "interdisciplinary circle" and what connection this exotic snake has with the unicorn.

29 June

With Gaby Gouillard from 4:00 till 10:00 (but she and Christinel went shopping, and then the two of them talked for some two hours). We hadn't seen her since Jean's funeral, exactly one year ago. I find out much about his last illness and about her desperate situation (without a pension because they were not "officially married" except for four years—although everyone knew that it would have been impossible earlier because Gaby's husband wouldn't give her a divorce).

I want to note here a detail from their last trip to Romania (Jean was participating in a conference of historians). The government, probably, had been obliged to accept a certain number of Bibles from England. Very soon after that, patrons of the larger hotels (participants at conferences, but also others) found pages torn from Bibles substituting for toilet tissue in the water closets.

12 July

Because Kenneth Woodward's article about me (''A Scholar's Sacred Quest'') appeared in the July fifteenth issue of *Newsweek,* I bought the magazine and read it from cover to cover. Depressing, saddening. You read about nothing but the success of terrorists (in Libya, Nicaragua, etc.), about revolutions, massive exterminations, the progress of the Soviets, and other things of the sort.

I congratulate myself once again for having decided twenty-five years ago not to read newspapers. I content myself with reading the headlines of the latest news. Sometimes Christinel ''briefs'' me on news items she has heard on television. In any case, I always *know* if something important or grave has happened. And as soon as a ''crisis'' is declared, I buy and read several newspapers per day. The rest of the time, I have at least this consolation: that I'm not poisoning my life every day by perusing the morning papers.

13 July

At 4:30 Alexandru Rosetti comes to see me. He climbs the stairs slowly, using a cane for support. Deeply moved, we embrace; we haven't seen each other for several years. In the meantime, the professor has been ill: last winter he nearly died from the cold in his room in Bucharest—it was a miracle he survived. He was taken to a hospital where he stayed for three weeks (because it was heated!). He's thinner, one shoulder seems stooped, and he is almost deaf—his son can't always make him understand what I say to him. True, he's almost ninety. . . .

He shows me the pilot copy of his latest book (studies in general linguistics). He tells me about the young philosophers and historians in the homeland; although they don't hold good professorships, some of these young people are exceptional; he cites me names. He seems enthusiastic also over the ''Golescu Project,'' the publication of the encyclopedic dictionary of Iordache Golescu [1768–1848] (forty-five hundred pages in manuscript, which has been lying in the Library of the Romanian Academy for a century, and which no one has been able to consult).

After he leaves, impossible for me to continue working: this could well be our last meeting. It is to him, Al. Rosetti, that I owe my life and liberty. The tremendous good he did from 1938 on, for scores of writers, historians, savants.

14 July

I have read with great interest *La Vie de Alexandra David-Neel,* by Jean Chalon—especially for the documents reproduced: letters to her husband, confessions, etc.

I remembered the first book of hers I read: *Voyage d'une Parisienne à Lhassa.* From Chalon's biography I learn many details about the exceptional difficulties of other travellers in Asia. The extraordinary physical stamina and *will* of this woman! And yet, how commonplace her reflections on Buddhism seemed to me on first reading (and now as well), not to mention her anti-Christian and theosophical banalities.

But the example of Alexandra David-Neel's *life* is almost without equal. What an excellent subject for a novel! A great artist, a lover of music, fascinated by freedom, and drawn into innumerable "experiences" so rare at the end of the nineteenth century—perceiving the importance of Tibet and Central Asia, shielded from fate (by the sums her husband—who remained at home—sent her with regularity), profiting by several exceptionally favorable historical circumstances, having the good luck to lecture about her travels in all centers of culture, and revealing ultimately "truths" which an educated reader would have discovered for himself by reading volumes available to all at Musée Guimet!

EYGALIÈRES, *15 July*

This morning, before leaving for the station, I received some copies of *Actes du Colloque International d'Aix en Provence, 3–5 May, 1948: Mircea Eliade et les horizons de la culture.* A book of more than three hundred pages, whose table of contents attracts me immediately. I believe I'll read it (something I don't do very often). In any event, I've taken a few copies along with me.

We left for Avignon at 3:40 and arrived at 7:00. For the first time the sky becomes dark before we reach Lyon, and at the Avignon station a drizzling rain begins to fall. Ileana greets us, laughing; for years our car has always been at the front of the train, far from the platform; this time it was the last. She was afraid we'd missed the train.

Curious how this banal detail fascinates me. It's as though it were the beginning of a novella; or even more interesting, a *sign* that's been made to me (as usual—at least, this is my conviction—the most profound mysteries and revelations are camouflaged in commonplace events). Of course, I don't allude to this obsessing fascination.

When we gather on the terrace in front of the house (Maria is here too), I am suffused with an almost inconceivable feeling of peace. I gaze fascinated at the centuries-old linden tree (as if I were seeing it for the first time), I listen melancholically to the cicadas.

16 July

Have read with great interest the first two studies in *Actes,* about my novels. Both well informed; many original observations.

18–29 July

Simply extraordinary days. The sky has remained as clear as it was the evening we arrived. Warm, but never oppressively hot or humid. A breeze; one day only the mistral; the evenings rather cool, so that we have need of a light sweater.

I've worked every day, at least four or five hours. Secluded in the tower, surrounded by the books and encyclopedias collected by Ioan in order to have them handy in his old age. And Ileana adds to them continually other books and new editions of classics.

Have corrected and transcribed the last fifteen pages of the *Autobiography,* written in Palm Beach last January. I've succeeded in writing another ten pages, and I've persisted in transcribing them—lest they become invisible (I'm writing with a pencil).

PARIS, *July*

I must admit it: in actuality, I'm doing nothing. That is, although I'm working five or six hours every day, I don't succeed in finishing anything. Since I arrived in Paris, I've started many things: the restoration of the Romanian text of *Fragments d'un journal* I, the final correcting of the *Journal* for 1982-1985, the preparation of the last chapter for *Histoire* IV, and other, lesser things.

Sometimes I have the impression that I'm threatened by a fast-working senility. I feel detached from all I've loved heretofore: philosophy, the history of religions, literature. I console myself (or I *try* to) as best I can. I tell myself the last treatments have tired me.

1 August

The days pass, and, unfortunately, the last months allowed to me are flowing by—while I do nothing. Fatigue, yes, but especially *indifference*. I have so many things to do that I know that in no event will I be able to do them all. I'd like, nevertheless, to continue the *Autobiography* and to write the last chapter of *Histoire* IV—and I *must*, at all costs, prepare the preface for the *Encyclopedia of Religion*. But if I keep putting things off. . . .

22 August

For three days in Paris—my cousin Ginu and his wife Sabina. I haven't seen Ginu in fifty years. He is the son of my "favorite" aunt, Lina. She died very young of tuberculosis—as did also her sisters Viorica, Vita, and Marioara.

I knew long ago, from Corina, that Ginu "admired" me, that he had read all my works that he could find in the homeland. For several years he has been retired. Finally, this summer, he obtained a passport—and he has come for the first time to the West. They stayed first for a few weeks in Amsterdam with Sorin.

24 August

Mircea Handoca has come, this time with his wife. I see him again after, I believe, fourteen or fifteen years. I remember how badly I treated him then. I hardly opened my mouth. A half hour before he came I had learned of "Titel" Comarnescu's fatal illness: cancer of the liver, metastasis.

Of course, I don't recognize him. He's fifty-six, but looks older. He brings me, among other things, copies of old letters from Cioran and

Dinu Noica to me, and one from Eugène Ionesco from Călărași (1934, when he was doing his military service).

They will stay in Paris for two or three weeks, in order for him to investigate my correspondence here, and my manuscripts. He will be, probably, disappointed. In the boxes I have found very few manuscripts. As for the correspondence—rather interesting—it stops about 1953 (it begins in 1950); the rest is located, probably, in the trunk in Jacqueline's cellar. I stored the letters there, together with other materials—books, magazines—in 1951. Since then I haven't opened that huge trunk.

The news—rather indifferent. For four years no book of mine has been published. Now, several are "in process": articles about Eminescu, the first volume of my works of youth (manuscripts from the first years of lycée and articles published between 1921 and 1926). Quite justifiably, Christinel is indignant that such adolescent texts will be published instead of my *books*. Nevertheless, Noica and Handoca's viewpoint is not without interest. Noica says that these books could become *exemplary* for young people; they demonstrate how a lycéen, in those years after the war, 1921–1925, without books, without modern libraries, without the encouragement of his teachers—worked, did not let himself be overwhelmed by discouragement, and succeeded in becoming the student and savant of later.

29 August

Mircea Handoca. No need to describe everything. He searches for manuscripts and letters, which he photocopies. (For the expenses of this, I lend him three thousand francs.)

Probably because of this return to the past, I feel depressed, exhausted.

I reread the letter I wrote to Lucian Blaga, from Berlin, after we had spent a week together, invited to their boarding house in Berne. I kept repeating that *now* (in 1937!) some of his books of philosophy should be translated into German and French.

I cannot reconcile myself to the destiny of Lucian Blaga. What he was in that era, 1937–1940—and what he became a few years later.

Reduced to silence, with half a normal salary (at the university library), without a chair, without permission to travel or even to have contacts with the West. I think of myself: without that *felix culpa* (being a disciple of Nae Ionescu), I'd have remained in the homeland. At the best, I'd have died of tuberculosis in a prison.

August

I believe it would be useless and of no interest to set down here all the declines and deficiencies I've observed in myself recently. Lapses of memory (sometimes it's impossible to recall a famous name, the title of a favorite book, etc.; it doesn't come to me until several minutes later); the forgetting (real?) of certain arguments which I used freely in discussions of several years ago. No need to add tiredness, somnolence, detachment.

Of all my physical ills, which are multiplying (pains in the hands and arthritic attacks, myopia, tendinitis in the right ankle, pains recently in the left knee, etc.), the most grave, it seems to me, is the physical fatigue. I can't walk for more than half an hour. Then I have to sit down, exhausted, on a bench. This summer I've hardly walked at all in "our Paris": the Latin Quarter, boulevard St. Germain, and the surrounding area.

9 September

Fortunately, I read the newspapers only occasionally. But I keep hearing all the time about the same sort of events: juvenile acts of terrorism; acts of violence on trains, in subway stations, on the street; banks or supermarkets taken by storm, etc.

How fortunate are those who believe in "the end of the world"! They, at least, don't suffer from the almost total indifference of our contemporaries.

14 September

Edith Silbermann wrote to me last spring and then telephoned me in June here at Paris in connection with the hour she wants to devote to me on German television. I refused. Sigfried Unseld writes me today, proposing the same thing (I don't know if it's a matter of the same branch of the German television or not). I replied by telegraph that my health does not allow me such an effort—which is, in part, true. In the same way, I've refused in recent years I don't know how many proposals from French television (among others, "Apostrophe").

Probably some of my friends think I'm crazy—or irresponsible.

15 September

From the articles which Ioan Culianu has dedicated to me, I understand that in recent years the "methodological" criticisms brought against my conceptions of the history of religions have increased. The fault is, in part, mine; I've never replied to such criticisms, although I ought to have done so. I told myself that someday, "when I'm free from works in progress," I'll write a short theoretical monograph and explain the "confusions and errors" for which I am reproached.

I'm afraid I'll never have time to write it.

ROME, 23 September

We land at 6:00. Warm; clear sky. Directly to Hotel Plaza. Pufuleţ comes—and we eat dinner at the Capriciosa. A young couple— the man sings, accompanying himself on the guitar; the woman sings only American love songs and takes up donations in a tambourine— makes its way among the tables. Music from 1950; but there are also some songs I heard on my first trips to Italy in 1927 and 1928. Extraordinary impression. It's as though I were reliving my early youth, but also, for Christinel and me both, our first walks in Naples, Capri, Rome, and Venice. . . . But these returns into a beatific past are hard for Christinel to take. The tears well up, and finally she begins to cry. (I can guess why: she's remembering Sibylle, Mamy. . . .)

At 11:00 we go to bed, exhausted.

24 September

Warm, clear day. In a word, as Rome has rarely treated us. We have come here because, this summer, my editor, Sante Bagnoli, offered to take us for an auto trip to Orvieto and Spoleto. But we preferred to start with Rome, so we're spending a few days here.

I keep remembering Via della Scrofa, where I lived some two or three months in the spring of 1928. I'd like to see it again, with Christinel, on an afternoon—just the two of us. But at 1:30 we are both tired, and we lie down. We sleep an hour. Then Christinel goes to the Scala Santa. I am frightened at the thought of the stairs she'll be climbing—with the two scars from the hernia operations.

25 September

The weather remains the same: superb. But I feel tired after a walk of one kilometer. I keep wondering what can be the cause of this sudden weakness. The treatments I've had? Or old age (in which I refuse to believe)?

I keep telling myself that I *must take full advantage* of this vacation in Rome, in Italy. It could be my last. If the pains in the right ankle and those in the left knee should get worse, any walking would be out of the question.

26 September

Curious, but I have no desire to see my colleagues and friends at Rome again: Mario Bussagli, Gnoli, and the others. There aren't many left. The most recent to go: Horia Roman and Giuseppe Tucci. And before them, Mircea Popescu, R. Pettazzoni.

I knew long ago that Rome no longer is the same—the Rome of my early youth, or of the years when I came here with Christinel, invited by Pettazzoni, Tucci, and Giacomo.

This evening Christinel and I dine alone at the Nino.

27 September

Superb weather. But, unfortunately, I feel tired. The same mysterious somnolence after lunch.

Nevertheless, we get as far as Piazza Colonna. So many memories. A few minutes in the Rizzoli Bookstore. But almost nothing interests me anymore. (In the old days, as soon as I'd arrive in Italy I'd go to a bookstore and ask about the latest book by Papini, the most recent publications in the history of religions, etc.) And yet, Rome remains just as fascinating, although Christinel and I are walking its streets alone.

But today we reached the hotel with difficulty. After a few hundred yards, I felt exhausted. We went upstairs to our room, and I slept an hour. I believe I'm over the tiredness, but I don't have any desire to do anything. (I should have answered several letters.)

A novella begins to come to me in this huge lobby of the hotel, where I like to rest with a cup of coffee and a glass of mineral water. The novella: someone returns here after ten or fifteen years. But I don't know anything else.

Trying to carry the novella further, I find myself "caught" by another subject, one having to do with my suspicious somnolence. An autobiographical novella, in fact. About a writer who, working mostly at night, suffers from insomnia, in spite of all the sleeping tablets he takes. Like any writer, he continues to be obsessed by the characters he discovers and describes. Once it happens that one of his secondary characters, from a novella already written—many years before, in fact—reproaches the author for making light of him, for describing him hastily and superficially, for the fact that, actually, he didn't understand the novella and had concluded it abruptly, although he could have continued it—because only then did it begin to become interesting.

I break off the summary here. I'll starting writing on loose pages.

ORVIETO, *28 September*

Sante Bagnoli comes to get us at exactly 3:30. In less than three hours we are in Orvieto. We have a room reserved at that charming Hotel Marino, a few hundred yards from the Piazza of the Dome, Santa Eufemia. Extraordinary impression, now, when the sun has almost set. The façade: one can't get enough of looking at it. And yet the body of the cathedral belongs to another style: Roman. Unnecessary to praise the purity and perfection of the whole. Each column is decorated with a different design. And close to the altar, on the right, is an amazing room with paintings by Luca Signorelli—the sacred history, from the creation of Adam to scenes in Hell. Finally, at age seventy-eight, I am granted to see the *original* of these famous Signorelli frescoes!

Useless to record other observations. Astonished by the syncretistic character of the cathedral: Roman style, with a pre-Baroque façade.

The square is full of children who are playing right beside the cathedral walls, and of couples and groups of young people who, obviously, are tourists. We walk a little (because I'm not allowed to tire myself!) on streets which still retain their medieval structures. Sante has reserved a table for us at the Molino Restaurant, which belongs to our hotel. But we cross a good part of the city before we find it. Excellent, from all points of view. At a certain moment we find ourselves discussing the theology of present-day Catholic politics. I realize that during this trip we've been in conversation almost all the time: on the subject of Japan (from which Sante returned a few days ago); on the magazine, *Umana Avventura*, which will appear simultaneously in four languages; and others. Maybe that's the cause of my fatigue and, especially, the somnolence which has exasperated me this past week.

We returned to the hotel in the proprietor's car, of course.

SPOLETO, *29 September*

This morning, after breakfast, I find Sante in the salon. He shows me a superb book on medieval art which Jaca Book will release soon. Too precious for me to leaf through now; too heavy (several kilograms?) for us to take with us. He will send it to me in Paris.

I admired several churches in Orvieto, but only one was open. Christinel is happy that we can light candles and pray for many of our friends.

Toward noon we leave for Spoleto. How amazing Umbria is! And we scarcely know it.

We cross Spoleto with difficulty. Opposite the cathedral we stop; obviously, it's closed. But we sit down at a table, order a sandwich apiece, and look at it. No need to remember the streets we drove along. I was thinking of something else entirely. Amusing details I had heard concerning the festival at Spoleto. But also unexpected details from the novella I "saw" a few days ago.

Nevertheless, I feel tired. The sentiment that I've arrived here too late.

Sante takes us slowly down from the hill of the medieval city, and after a two-hour ride in the automobile, a surprise: the town of Torgiana and the extraordinary hotel, Le Tre Vasolli. Extraordinary indeed. A superb, lordly dwelling, connected, underground, to several buildings on the other side of the street. Everything—the architecture, furniture, etc.—in perfect taste. We visit several large rooms where lectures are given. At 8:00 P.M. Roberto Mussapi arrives (by train, from Milan). Dinner lasts a long time. Sante is determined, at all costs, to taste at least two famous wines: Torre de Giano and Rubesco.

TODI-ROME, *30 September*

This morning we visit the unique Museo del Vino. Discussions, beginning in the hotel and continuing in the car.

We see Todi at a distance. I remember my first readings of Jacopone da Todi, in adolescence, and I tell them about my puzzlement. Then my mind reverts to the novella, and I don't know how to explain to the others my sudden silences.

We arrive at the Palace Square, and Sante succeeds in parking the car close to that great parapet from which one can see all of Umbria. Short walk in the piazza. Christinel climbs the sixty or eighty steps of the cathedral. Fortunately, the service ends just then, and she is able to go inside.

We arrive at Hotel Plaza at sunset. Unfortunately, the new room which has been given us is small, uncomfortable, and noisy: we can hear constantly a low, metallic sound like that of an elevator (and yet it's something else, because the noise continued, without interruption, all night).

In the evening the two of us dined with Pufuleţ at the Capricioso.

ROME, *1 October*

Terrible night. We hardly slept a wink. Today Christinel succeeds in getting our room changed.

Tired, in low spirits, I wait for Mussapi, for the promised interview. He comes at 2:00 with a small tape recorder, but he assures me that I'll be able to review the text in a few days. The theme: the role of poetry.

It will appear in the first volume of the *Poetry Annual* which Roberto is publishing. He ends the interview at 3:30, and then we keep talking for an hour or so about literature, especially modern and contemporary poetry. Curious reactions: Mussapi adores Beckett but doesn't like Ionesco; he is fascinated by Ion Barbu, though he has read him only in mediocre Italian and French translations.

From discussions with him and Bagnoli, I realize how forgotten are Papini, Panzini, and E. Buonaiuti (I proposed that he republish at least a few of Buonaiuti's smaller works—on the origins of Christian asceticism, G. da Fiore, etc.), not to mention D'Annunzio and the other "classics." On the other hand, he is going to publish a monograph on Ernesto de Martino. Sante is fascinated by all I tell him about de Martino, in particular his extraordinary assertion, which exasperated Croce (his great protector): that "nature is culturally conditioned." What a fascinating *physical world* we would live in if de Martino were right! (I ought to write an article on this theme.)

This evening, invited to the Toto by Nicola and Nina, together with Şerban and Ninuska. I hadn't seen Şerban for a good many years. He has a beard; he completed his collection of postage stamps of the Vatican in 1975; he hopes to become an aerial navigator in 1986 or 1987. With me he likes to speak English.

2 October

The weather continues as it was the first days: superb. I haven't seen a cloud in the sky.

At noon, seated on a bench in Piazza di Spagna. At 1:00 the school children begin to emerge—from the primary classes up to the last class of lycée. I am fascinated by the variety of book bags hanging from backs and shoulders: of all shapes (pouches, little knapsacks, etc.) and colors. As in Paris, many girls light cigarettes as soon as they step out of the lycée door.

Impossible for me to concentrate on the novella. I know we're leaving for the airport at 6:00.

Epilogue

Wendy Doniger

This is an extraordinarily vivid and touching book about old age, a totally unstructured, almost surreal portrait of the disintegrating world of a great intellectual, the Indian summer of a great man of letters. The Eliade that we encounter in this book is a man who tries in vain to stop the inevitable advance of death's glacier by throwing in its path words, words, words: papers, books, articles, articles about books, reviews, responses to reviews, encyclopedias about books, letters, replies to letters, reviews of encyclopedias about books, and on and on and on. And, participating in the play within the play, we the readers enter into a small fraction of that massive arsenal of self-reflections (datebooks, journals, autobiographies).

The book reveals the two mutually contradictory aspects of Eliade's literary agony: the problem of creating, and the problem of destroying. On the one hand, he is constantly writing, or, more often, trying in vain to write: "A good day: I wrote twenty pages." "Today I could only write six pages, and I fear they were quite mediocre." His writing is his salvation from life, and when he cannot write, he cannot live. Near the end, he experiences exhaustion and depression; but then suddenly he has a wonderful vision for a new novella, and in the next few days his mind keeps reverting to the novella, even in the middle of conversations with others, who are puzzled. On almost every page of the book, literally, he expresses his anguish at his mounting inability to read or, far more infuriating for him, to write all that he still hopes to finish, crippled as he is by his steadily decaying vision and the pain and paralysis of his arthritic hands. Annoying at first, these repetitions gradually take on a kind of insistent and convincing rhythm and make us feel what he feels: frustration, the conviction that nothing he writes is as good as he wants it to be, that he is getting nothing finished even though he works all the time.

The other horn of this dilemma is what he conceives as the problem of getting rid of what he has already written (an enormous corpus) and what he has collected that others have written. (also enormous): the problem of disposing of his library. He was overpowered by the feeling that he must do something, get the papers safe, give away the books, before the end came: "I still have to give away (to the library, friends, students), some three thousand books. . . . Only then will I have space on my shelves for *my* books, manuscripts, and correspondence, the theses and studies about me, etc." "How I dread to receive and open *now* packages of books. . . . in anticipation of a 'liquidation' (for Regenstein?). . . ." His feverish planning about whom to give his books and papers is reminiscent of a rich old uncle gathering his nephews around him to tell them what they will have; it is also reminiscent of the beginning of *King Lear*. Thus on 25 May, 1982, after writing about giving away his books to various people, he remarks, "I don't quite understand why I felt the need to write this note. It would have been more useful for me to make a list of the persons I'm thinking of. But such exercises depress me quickly. . . ." He worries about how to dispose of his books because he is haunted by a fear that they will be destroyed somehow before he can dispose of them, a fear that turned out to be a true premonition.

These two antipodal literary obsessions, an ironic *coincidentia oppositorum,* recur on almost every page of the diary, balancing one another, teasing one another, tearing one another apart. For in this book, the primary focus is books; people come second. Even when something real happens to him, he reconceives it as a literary event. A dinner at a famous hotel leads him to wish, "I should like, someday, to have one of my novella characters live in that hotel." Apparently he does not aspire to live in the hotel himself, as a nonwriter might have wished. When he learns of the death of his old friend Tucci, the great Tibetologist, he remarks, "Terrible sadness . . . Memories: the first meeting in Dasgupta's house in Bhowanipore, in the winter of 1929, and all that followed. How I regret having lost *The Journal* from those years! (Perhaps it will be discovered later, but what good will that do?). . . ." The loss of the man is quickly transmuted into the loss of the man's writings. Eliade betrays the priority of paper over flesh in statements such as this: "Formerly, that is, twenty or thirty years ago, the more things I had to do (to write), the better I did them, and the more quickly." How easily "to do" becomes "to write."

Since books constituted this lifeline for Eliade, he regarded the destruction of his books as a significant and ominous sign that his own death was not far off. When his library in his office in the Meadville-Lombard School of Religion was destroyed by fire, on 19 December 1985, just four months before he died (on April 22, 1986), the following note was found on his desk in his apartment, written on the morning after the fire:

> Last night, at ten o'clock, I heard someone knocking at our door. Our neighbor, from the floor below, tells me: "Your office's on fire! . . . I telephoned the fire department. They've been working there for five minutes. Maybe you'd better come and see what's happened."
>
> I dressed as fast as I could and went with him. I heard the firemen breaking the windows of my office. It was terribly cold, and the water flowing down the stairs of Meadville froze as soon as it reached the sidewalk.
>
> They wouldn't let me go in. On the main stairs the water was pouring down like a mountain stream.
>
> So it began. I had to go back home. Christinel gave me a double dose of sleeping tablets.[1]

There is much to be read in this short statement. When I asked Eliade why he was so saddened by the burning of his library, since most of it consisted of copies of the books that he himself had written, books that were still in print and could therefore be replaced, he told me that they were specially annotated copies: after their initial publication, he had kept making notes in his copies of them, keeping the books alive, up to date, changing them to fix them and to correct their errors, to add new thoughts that he had continued to have on those subjects and to expand the bibliographies when other scholars continued to publish related works, often in response to those very books of his. In doing this, Eliade was keeping the books in history, as it were, keeping them alive and changing. And when those books were burnt, he felt that all the years of continued growth had been erased. The books that he had dragged forward with him into the future were, overnight, transported back in time to the moment at which they had been published. The books had, in a very real sense, returned to their origins, to the moment of their birth; and this was not what he had wanted. The immortality that he had sought on the printed page was subject to material destruction, just like the immortality that he had once, long ago, sought in his experiments with yoga. The fire put an end to the history of the books, prevented their history from progressing, stopped them at the moment of their publication. In neither life nor literature could time be conquered. This was an unexpected foretaste of a death more shattering than the expected death of the body.

Eliade's journal entries for the last years of his life reveal an almost obsessive premonition that his library would be destroyed and, with it, his life. His sense of the fragility and impermanence of the written word was all-pervasive: ''This morning I try to put the finishing touches to some notes from Yucatan; I wrote with a pencil in great haste, and they would have become completely illegible in a week's time.'' And later: ''In Chicago I collected a large number of notes and observations in an envelope . . . I leaf through it with melancholy: more than half the pages written are illegible to me now.'' On one occasion, he records his recurrent dream of the destruction of a library. On another occasion, worried about what he should do about all his books and papers, he writes: ''*Anything* could happen, at any time.'' And: ''Only today did I realize that my Monier-Williams Sanskrit dictionary has disappeared.

When? I consulted it the last time in May. Who could have taken it? Almost anyone can enter my office. . . ." After giving away some of his books, he writes: "I have also the sentiment that I am anticipating the 'breaking up' which will take place after my death."

His belief that his work was, in a sense, more important than his life might have been expected to make him more, rather than less, patient about his degenerating physical condition and his impending death; his books, after all, would go on living after him. But he did not see it that way; as he saw it, the hand crippled with arthritis was not merely a wretched mass of aching nerves and petrified tendons, but the recalcitrant instrument of a sacred task: "I must continue 'my work' (that is, what I was predestined to do), despite all the infirmities which are continually multiplying: loss of memory, worsening of the myopia, physical fatigue, arthritic pains, and above all the immense difficulty of writing legibly."

Yet time and time again he wrenched himself out of his narrow frustrations with his own literary projects and into a broader vision of what awaited him at the end of the task; or, as he himself would have put it, he raised his gaze from the profane to the sacred: "I feel worse and worse; drowsy, no desire to work, tired. I'm sure that the treatment with gold isn't agreeing with me. I have no more pain, but my right hand remains as stiff as before. I write with enormous difficulty. In addition, the cataract has progressed. I hardly manage to read: I can do better without the glasses, holding my face almost against the page. And in spite of everything, I persist in believing in the 'initiatory' meaning of these sufferings and debilities. I'm not thinking of death. At my age, that's no longer a problem. The 'initiation' pertains to *something else:* a 'new life,' i.e., a total regeneration which reveals to me another kind of creativity. I must get out of this pen of petty preoccupations in which I've been enclosed, without realizing it, for so many years." At such moments, he was able to regard as "petty preoccupations" not only the physical problems of his last years and his frustrated final attempts to complete his work, but even his long-standing, single-minded devotion to that work.

Yet he always fell back into his obsession with his own books and his own past, with the desperate effort to record the quarter decade that he spent in Chicago, with the writing and publishing of the endless journals of which the present document is the final manifestation. Finally, he acknowledges this: "I realize now the great mistake I made: instead of 'classifying' my correspondence for Regenstein's Special Collections, I ought to have worked on the pages of the *Autobiography* already written and continued Chapter 20. But, I admit, I was fascinated—and paralyzed—by that disinterment of my past: those twenty-five years spent in Chicago." And once, when Christinel was in the hospital and he was alone, "I can't work. The same old story: I'm living among the letters and notes of twenty and twenty-five years ago."

On 21 July, 1979, he records a dream:

I leave home with the manuscript of a study on which I had worked several months, to make a photocopy of it. I come to a strange garden or park in the vicinity of the office where the manuscript is to be photocopied. A well-dressed man is there, with many small animals around him. I don't know why, but I fold the manuscript and press it together, reducing it to the size of a sandwich, and try, for fun, to threaten a little rat with it. But the animal takes hold of the packet with his mouth and won't let go. Although he isn't biting or chewing it, I observe that the manuscript is getting smaller. Impossible to pull it out of the rat's mouth. I have nothing handy with which to hit it. Alarmed, I beg the elegant gentleman, who is standing directly in front of me, to stab the rat. He replies that *here* he does not have the right to fire a revolver (?). I watch desperately as my manuscript disappears. Very soon there is nothing left in my hand but a narrow strip of paper, a few millimeters wide. Only then does the rat let loose of it—and he goes away. I was desperate. I had lost an important text on which I had worked many months; and I hadn't saved any notes, not even the note cards. . . . I started toward the office of the photocopier, at my wits' end. Fortunately, a few moments later I woke up. But for a long time I couldn't go back to sleep. I realized that the dream constituted a ''message,'' but I didn't succeed in deciphering it.

If I may rush in where he refused to tread, it seems to me that this powerful dream is quite clear at least in its broad outlines, which evoke the nightmares of many if not all writers. But since it was Eliade who dreamed it, it may well have incorporated a famous Indian parable that he knew well, a story in which a man is hanging by a thin thread that is being gnawed by a rat; the rat is Time, and the thread is the man's unrealized line of descent, for he has no children. In support of this partial gloss I cite the journal entry in which, despairing of disposing of his library as he wishes, Eliade remarks, ''How simple it would be if we had had *heirs,* if Sibylle had lived, or Ioan Cuşa. . . .'' The books are the children that he never had.

His final journal entry, in Rome on October 2, 1985, ties together all of these themes. It is about books, children, his inability to go on writing, and his imminent departure on what was to be his last journey, to Chicago and beyond:

The weather continues as it was the first days: superb. I haven't seen a cloud in the sky. At noon, seated on a bench in Piazza di Spagna. At 1:00 the school children begin to emerge—from the primary classes up to the last class of lycée. I am fascinated by the variety of book bags hanging from backs and shoulders: of all shapes (pouches, little knapsacks, etc.) and colors. As in Paris, many girls light cigarettes as soon as they step out of the lycée door. Impossible for me to concentrate on the novella. I know we're leaving for the airport at 6:00.

Index